PATRICK EGBERUARE

PATHWAY TO PEACE, FORGIVENESS & RECONCILIATION

Pathway to Peace, Forgiveness & Reconciliation
Copyright © 2020 by Patrick Egberuare. All rights reserved.

No part of this publication may be reproduced, stored in a retrieval system or transmitted in any way by any means, electronic, mechanical, photocopy, recording or otherwise without the prior permission of the author except as provided by USA copyright law.

This book is designed to provide accurate and authoritative information with regard to the subject matter covered. This information is given with the understanding that the author is not engaged in rendering legal or professional advice. Since the details of your situation are fact dependent, you should additionally seek the services of a competent professional.

Names: Egberuare, Patrick, author.

Title: Pathway to peace, forgiveness & reconciliation / Patrick Egberuare

Book design copyright © 2020 by Patrick Egberuare Ministries.
All rights reserved.

Published in the United States of America

ISBN: 978-0-578-76359-0

1. Social Justice / Peace
2. Political Science / International Relations / General

SPECIAL SALES
Books are available at special quantity discounts for bulk purchases by corporations, organizations, and special groups. For information please e-mail gpff1990@gmail.com

DEDICATION

THIS BOOK IS dedicated to all those who believe in the triple heritage of peace, forgiveness, and reconciliation in Nigeria, America and other parts of the globe.

ACKNOWLEDGMENTS

FOR HIS ENABLING grace, divine wisdom, and the vision for the writing of this book, the Almighty God takes the prime position in my expression of appreciation and gratitude.

I acknowledge and gratefully express my profound appreciation to all the noble people who had made one contribution or the other to the success of this project.

To members of the Global Peace and Forgiveness Foundation in Nigeria, who believe in making the world a better place, you are a part of the hope of the world by contributing your quota to world peace.

To my mentors at Dream City Church, Pastor Luke Barnett

and his dad, Pastor Tommy Barnett, whom I have garnered a lot from, I am deeply grateful for the impact of your ministries over my life and ministry.

To ALPHAGRAPHICS, your entire team's dedication to this project will always be mentioned.

And finally, to my lovely wife Blessing Egberuare, for her immense support, and our children: Dr. Emmanuel Egberuare, Overcomer Egberuare, Winner Egberuare, and Marvellous Egberuare, for their understanding of what it means to be true ambassadors of peace; starting from the family.

CONTENTS

FOREWORD

Today, the world is facing serious challenges of managing wars, terrorism, and conflicts. Enormous resources needed for development and improvement of lives of people are diverted to conflict resolution, war on terrorism, and settlement of displaced peoples and refugees. The world surely needs peace and security in order to face squarely, the serious issues of development.

Qualitative development can only be produced under a conducive political atmosphere. It therefore stands to believe that some of the major obstacles to development of the world are the presence of many needless conflicts, wars, armed struggles etc, in many countries of the World.

In the West Africa subregion in the last twenty years, conflicts and wars have claimed thousands of lives and huge resources. That is the primary reason that poverty, sickness, and diseases are prevalent in the subregion. World leaders spend more time travelling from one country to another, meeting on how to resolve conflicts than they spend on critical issues of delivering good governance and development to their people.

The big question is- How long are we going to continue like this?

It is certain that no meaningful progress can be made in an atmosphere of strife, war, conflicts and suspicion. We must resolve, as human beings, to live in peace, to accommodate one another, to respect the feelings of others, to build friendship, to demonstrate love, and show forgiveness. This, we should start from the family level to our immediate environment, to our local community, and to the wider society.

Our attitude to others must be influenced by profound understanding that the world around us can only survive and make progress through our actions, no matter how insignificant they may appear to us. We must always be conscious of the cumulative effects, which our actions and inactions can have on the lives of the people around us, whether as ordinary citizens or leaders.

Today, in the face of daunting challenges of poverty, strange diseases, wars, terrorism, crimes of unimaginable proportions, the world needs peace more than ever. And it is the duty of every individual to contribute to the sustenance of world peace.

Professor Jerry Gana

VISIT MY VALLEY OF VISION

"Where there is no vision the people perish."
—King Solomon

MANY YEARS AGO, as a gospel missionary evangelist in Nigeria, I was far away in Taraba State, Nigeria when I came face-to-face with the perennial conflicts that had engulfed the Fulanis and the Mambillas, the Tivs and the Jukuns, the Kutebs and the Chambas, the Mumuyes and the Fulanis, the Wurukuns and the Fulanis at different fronts.

The crises I witnessed amongst the abovementioned Nigerians shocked me to the marrow, and I had to seek divine intervention. It was when I started praying, the Lord began to speak to me concerning the urgent need for peace in Nigeria.

As I reflected on the fratricidal fighting from all fronts in the northeastern lowlands of Taraba, I could not help but remember similar sad episodes in different parts of an otherwise well-blessed country. I thought of the many lives, goods, and property that had been lost in ethnic confrontations not only in Taraba State, but in the southwestern parts of Osun and Ondo States where the Ifes and the Modakekes, the Akures and Idanres never seem to agree.

I remembered the cat and mouse existence between the Umuleri and Aguleri in southeastern state of Anambra and between the Anangs and Ibibios in Akwa Ibom. I sighed over the hostilities in Kaduna State, over the introduction of sharia laws, which nearly plunged Nigeria into her second civil warfare, with all its frightening proportions. I cried over the bellicosity in Jos, Plateau State, hitherto most peaceful city in Nigeria, where ethno-religious combats have been creating doubts in the minds of most optimists who still believe in the cooperate existence of Nigeria.

Need I mention the communal contentions between the Itsekiris and Urhobos in the Niger Delta?

What of the peace lost in Edo, in Ogoni land, in Shedam, in Wase, in Nassarawa, in Gombe, in Benue, in Kogi, in all Nigeria? The more one thinks about the flash points in Nigeria, the more one remembers the historical records of the Dark Ages when human life was considered brutish, short, and inconsequential because of man's inhumanity to man. But Nigeria is not the only country in the world where pockets of crises tend to threaten peaceful coexistence.

In fact, when we think in global terms, we cannot help but remember most African countries, especially Liberia, Sierra Leone, Angola, Algeria, Democratic Republic of Congo (former Zaire), Burundi, Rwanda, Somalia, North Sudan, South Sudan, Uganda, Niger, Namibia, Botswana, Mozambique, South Africa, Zimbabwe, Cote d'Ivoire, and so on, as countries where ethnic tensions and civil wars had rocked to their foundations at one time or the other.

Outside the African continent, the political conflicts and potential wars in the Middle East, especially between the Israelites and the Palestinians, stare the world in the face with horrifying implications.

Equally disturbing, the sabre-rattlings in many Arab nations, such as Afghanistan, Pakistan, Iraq, Iran, Tunisia, Syria, Libya, Islamabad, etc., testify to the fact, that part of the world is not free from cross swords.

Likewise, the world is aware, that in Asia, the two Koreas are at daggers drawn, while India and Pakistan have known no peace both internally and externally, individually and between themselves, over Kashmir. The Hindus and Muslims are rocking India internally, while the Talibans are against the America-friendly government in Pakistan.

In Mexico, Central America, the Caribbean, and South America, we do know that Belize, Guatemala, Honduras, Panama, Nicaragua, Costa Rica, El Salvador, Bahamas, Cuba, Haiti, Jamaica, Dominican Republic, Grenada, Guyana, Venezuela, Colombia, Ecuador, Peru, Brazil, Chile, Argentina, Uruguay, Bolivia, Suriname, and French Guiana, are suffering from internal combustion, if not external aggression, because of political and economic asphyxia.

Even the developed nations of the world are not exempted from the "acquired immune deficiency" of internal sedition, alienation, separation, and fracas. For example, in the United States of America, the racial inequality between the whites and the blacks is a showcase of shame on Uncle Sam's pretensions to freedom and civilization. The clamor for racial justice after the tragic death of a black man George Floyd, by a white Police officer in Minneapolis, who knelt on his neck for nearly nine minutes is unmasking enough. This incident triggered worldwide protest as a result of the video of his horrific death, causing global outrage against police brutality and systemic racism across the globe.

Racial disharmony is a longstanding and deeply troubling problem despite claims that the United States has entered a "post-racial era." It occurs frequently in cities and states across the country. Let us not forget the words of former President Ronald Reagan. "For we must consider that we shall be as a city upon a hill. The eyes of all people are upon us. So that if we shall deal falsely with our God in this work we have undertaken, and so cause Him to withdraw His present help from us, we shall be made a story and a by-word through the world."

In Great Britain, the strained relationship between the British and the Irish puts a terrible stain on the Union Jack. In Continental Europe, the repercussions of ethnic cleansing between Croatia, Bosnia and Herzegovina on one hand, and between the Russian Federation and Chechnya on the other hand, have exhausted the patience and endurance of lovers of peace all over the world.

I shed tears as these sad events and many more across the world, reeled across my mind.

The bothering questions are:

Can the world know peace?

Can the nations [people] of the world learn to forgive each other, and make *reconciliation possible*?

What must we do to bring about peace, forgiveness, and reconciliation in our world today?

The burdens for peace, forgiveness, and reconciliation are too heavy for one person to bear alone. Hence, there is every need for all hands to be on deck. The task is urgent, and peace lovers must rise in unison to work consciously for peace, where there is panic; for dialogue, where there are daggers; for justice, where there is inequity; for forgiveness, where there is misunderstanding; for reconciliation, where there is fracas; for prayer, where there is problem; for stability, where there is instability, and for true religion, where there is hypocrisy. My vision is to promote peace, forgiveness, and reconciliation, across the globe.

As you visit my valley of vision, let your humanity shine through to think more on the positive value of peace, justice, dialogue, forgiveness, reconciliation, prayer, stability, and faith to the end that God's word, "Be of good will to all men," will not be void in our time and clime on Planet Earth.

DIALOGUE WITHOUT DAGGERS

"Think like a wise man, but communicate in the language of the people."

—W. B. Yeats

IN OUR WIDE awake world of social intercourse, we engage in three different forms of conversation. These, we refer to as monologue, soliloquy, and dialogue. It's a sad fact that while most of us spend a sizeable part of our lives communicating with others— in face-to-face conversations, over the phone, in committee meetings, via e-mail and social networks — we seem to be more separated and disconnected than ever. Genuine understanding seems to be the exception rather than the norm in our everyday communication. We speak at each other, or past each other. We speak different conceptual languages, hold different values, and embody different ways of seeing the world.

The trouble with much of what passes for communication today is that it is all crosstalk. It is a din, not a dialogue. As we move into times of accelerating change and deepening uncertainty, we need to get smart about how to talk to one another. We need to be able to overcome differences, find common grounds, build meaning and purpose, and set directions together. We need to be able to talk together as groups, as teams, as committees, as communities, as nations and as one human race of this world. The way to do that is through dialogue. The word dialogue is often contrasted with monologue. While monologue refers to a long speech by one person, soliloquy means the act of talking to one's self. Dialogue, on the other hand, is a discussion between people in which opinions are exchanged.

Call it conversation. Call it confabulation. Call it discussion. Call it table talk. Call it rap. Call it debate. Call it what you will, but dialogue is a peaceful avenue through which sane people seek to express their opinions on a given matter. Dialogue makes it possible for people to talk without fighting. It is the civilized way to resolve conflicts.

The nations of the world are growingly recognizing the importance of mediation—dialogue without daggers. Apart from the high cost of war, dialogue is a preventive measure against the agonies of war. The high cost of war involves human and material resources, which nations at large can no longer afford to squander on battlefields.

Dialogue promotes civilization. Those who dialogue know that at the end of the day, they would have saved themselves and their nations a lot of headache, particularly when such dialogue (conference) leads to peaceful resolution of conflict or potential conflicts. The adage, "Prevention is better than cure," is as true in health matters, as it is in war situations. To allow situations to degenerate into irresolvable proportions, when with a little dialogue, solution and direction could be found, is to betray our sense of proper proportions and right relations.

Dialogue promotes peace. Once two parties agree to solve their misunderstanding amicably, the problem is half solved. Belligerence occurs when all doors are shut against dialogue on the lips of the belligerents. No peace can be secured without dialogue. Dialogue is therefore an important phase of human interaction.

But we must distinguish between constructive dialogue and dialogue of the deaf. Lord Chesterfield saw the importance of constructive dialogue when he said, "Never hold anyone by the button or the hand in order to be heard out for if people are unwilling to hear you, you had better hold your tongue than them." Constructive dialogue will achieve results while its counterfeit will fall on deaf ears. In the dialogue of the deaf, no one listens, no one hears. The dialogue of the deaf is like a noisy gong and clanging cymbals.

Those who believe in constructive dialogue will agree with Sir Winston Churchill, the former British prime minister, that the "further back you look, the further forward you are likely to see." History is more than the mere recording of events. It is hindsight, insight, and foresight. We must have these triple heritages if we are not to be consigned to the scrap heap of antediluvian era. We must be able to see ahead of an occurrence, that diplomacy will solve a lot of difficulties in human affairs. And it is better to apply tact, dialogue, and roundtable to reach a compromise on a thorny issue. A constructive dialogue can melt most of our common problems.

In his book titled *Ethnic Militias, Vigilantes and Separatist Groups in Nigeria*, Nnamdi K. Obasi has this to say: "The Nigeria society has, in recent years, witnessed an unprecedented proliferation of ethnic militias, vigilantes and separatist groups. Given the difference between these groups in terms of their origins, objectives, and modes of operation, their activities impact on several aspects of the Nigerian polity, society, and economy, and have far-reaching consequences for democracy, human security, and national unity." In fact, the foregoing reference is a mild way of saying ethnic militias, vigilantes, and separatist movements in Nigeria can threaten its corporate existence. In other words, if their activities are not carefully monitored, they can hold the nation to ransom. If they are not checked, they can check-mate its unity. If they are not disbanded, they will hijack the flower of our nation, and before you know it, plunge us into unprecedented mayhem.

Of course, the same group of people can be used to achieve dialogue on grey areas of common situations. But if they were ready for dialogue, they would not have resorted to the force of arms to advance their peculiar agenda. A better way out is to have a selected opinion leader, who are ever ready to dialogue with other ethnic nationalities, in the interest of the Nigerian nation.

Whether this can be achieved through elected representatives of people in the form of members of House of Representatives and Senators or through the convening of a national conference remains an open question. But we believe that the last two options present all stakeholders the choice of dialogue without daggers at resolving burning national issues.

The vision for a united, prosperous Nigeria can be sustained on durable dialogue whereby the citizens of Nigeria are ready to negotiate their welfare on a give-and-take basis. Here we need to emphasize that the three major ethnic groups in Nigeria—Hausa, Igbo, and Yoruba—need to show the way by engaging in dialogue on areas of differences, to enable other minority ethnic groups to follow suit. If Yoruba can talk with the Hausa-Fulani, if the Hausa- Fulani can talk with the Yoruba, and if the Igbo can talk with the Hausa and Yoruba on issues that will redound to the greater glory of Nigeria, there will be greater feelings of patriotism in them than it is presently, whereby staccato voices from their ethnic militias, vigilante groups, and separatist movements are clamoring for the bifurcation of the Nigerian state. The beauty of dialogue is that it gives room for ideas to flow in the marketplace. The better the ideas, the greater their chances for survival.

On a global dimension, more dialogue among world leaders has to be canvassed because it is urgently needed now more than ever. Those who pay lip service to world peace without taking steps to effecting it are just living in a world of delusion. They may shout peace, peace; but they will only hear war, war, for peace is a process of creating the right atmosphere. As Johann Wolfang von Goethe, the German philosopher puts it, "One man's word is no man's word. We should quietly hear both sides." To quote an American parlance, "To jaw, jaw is better than to war, war." To dialogue is superior to pointing daggers. To prevent war is easier than to end it.

The dynamics of verbal interchange are more beneficial to mankind than the arrows and daggers that waste by the noonday. The benefits of superior argument will advance the progress of the world rather than the sheer wastages of lives and property with guns and mortars. Amicable solutions to common problems are possible, provided there is mutual confidence.

The capacity to dialogue, to agree to disagree and to disagree to agree, is peculiarly human, and its frequent utilization will go a long way toward humanizing society, thereby making our world a better place to live. One of the main reasons that God made it possible for human beings to communicate is to enable them to dialogue. Let us utilize this divine asset for sustaining peace, justice, forgiveness, and reconciliation in our life time on the stage of life.

PEACE WITHOUT PANIC

"If we are to live in peace, we must come to know each other better."

—Lyndon B. Johnson

WRITING ON THE importance and efficacy of peace in a war torn world, F. Josephus has this to say, "Peace and good laws are the greatest blessings." J. W. Dickson, on the other hand, praises all promoters of peace in the following words, "All love and honor the apostles of peace, whose labors in the field of humanity elicit not only words of praise but plant within the bosom of all worthy souls the flower of brotherhood".

The universal, perennial question of why peace was once answered by a former peace-loving American president, Dwight D. Eisenhower, in the following way, "We seek peace, knowing that peace is the climate of freedom."

Why should we seek peace? We seek peace because peace offers the best opportunity for human expression. We seek peace because without it, there will be chaos and disruption of orderly existence of things. We seek peace because it is more comfortable and safer to live in peace, rather than catastrophe. We seek peace because peace advances human achievement and higher civilization.

We seek peace because it promotes the rapid development of cultural, religious, social, economic, political, and technological needs of man and nations. We seek peace because it builds up and sustains human existence, while war tears down and destroys human life and all that is noble. But above all, we seek peace because God commands man to be peaceful and to live at peace with his neighbor.

As the grand old book of the world, the Bible, puts it in the Old Testament:

> "Seek peace and pursue it (Psalm 34:14)."
>
> "I am for peace (Psalm 120:7)."
>
> "Behold, how good and pleasant it is for brethren to dwell together in unity (Psalm 133:1)."
>
> "To the counselors of peace is joy (Proverbs 12:20)."
>
> "When a man's ways please the Lord, he maketh even his enemies to be at peace with him (Proverbs 16:7)"

"It is an honor for a man to cease from strife: But every fool will be meddling (Proverbs 20:3)"

"He shall judge among the nations and shall rebuke many people: and they shall beat their swords into plowshares and their spears into pruning hooks: nation shall not lift up sword against nation, neither shall they learn war any more (Isaiah 2: 4)."

"I form the light and create darkness: I make peace…I, the Lord, do all these things (Isaiah 45:7)."

"Love the truth and peace (Zechariah 8:19)."

In the New Testament, the mother of books is no less succinct on the imperatives of peace:

"Blessed are the peacemakers for they shall be called the children of God (Matthew 5:9)."

"Have peace one with another (Mark 9:50)."

"Glory to God in the highest, and on earth, peace, goodwill toward men (Luke 2:14)."

"Let us therefore follow after the things which make for peace, and things where with we may edify another (Romans 14: 19)."

"Be perfect, be of good comfort, be of one mind, live in peace (2 Corinthians 13:11)."

"Endeavoring to keep the unity of the spirit in the bond of peace (Ephesians 4:3)."

"Be at peace among yourselves (1 Thessalonians 5:13)."

> "That we may lead a quiet and peaceable life in all godliness and honesty (1Timothy 2:2)."

> "Follow peace with all men, and holiness, without which no man shall see the Lord: Hebrew 12:14"

From the above rich scriptural references, it is abundantly clear that God loves peace. It is also evidently clear that God prefers peace to war. It further stated that God urges all men to live in peace, both with their creator and with themselves. In fact, one of the unique appellations ascribed to Jesus of Nazareth by Isaiah, the son of Amoz, is "Prince of Peace," not Hero of War!

War has done more damage to mankind than peace. A glance through the pages of history will confirm this. The First World War (1914–1918) was fought because European nations were power drunk, and they wanted to demonstrate their military prowess on the battlefield. Many lives were lost in this madness, yet they claim they fought to make the world safe for democracy. But the world was neither made safe for democracy nor did war abate.

The Second World War reared its horrid head in September 1939, and for the next six years, the nations of the world engaged themselves freely in a macabre dance of fighting to wipe out all wars from the face of the earth. Millions of souls perished in the shadow of death. Yet, after the Second World War, more nations of the world started stockpiling more weapons of destruction than ever before. While we may not necessarily go into the statistics of war machinery available to nations states herein, it is yet an open secret that nations of the North are now each capable of destroying the world many times over, just at the push of a button.

That, such a possibility is not remote should be viewed from the psychosomatic personality of Adolf Hitler, the Austrian-born, German-bred terrorist. In his war-mongering spirit to conquer Europe and bring the world under the feet of Germany, Hitler wasted the lives of over six million Jews in cold blood, in Gestapo concentration camps. The tragedy of this unmitigated disaster in human history is that a thousand repentances by all the Hitler's of the world today can never bring back the precious lives of the dead, whose blood will only continue to yearn for divine angst. Present day leaders of the world, who idolize Hitler, are simply not good students of history.

While still on war and its repercussions on human dignity, human psyche, and synergy, we need to look at some of the threats and imponderables to tranquility, and how we can overcome them before they overcome us and send us precipitously to kingdom come. Those who have sought for peace have come across many threats and barriers because of their beliefs, no matter how strong or feeble. Religious wars have been fought all over the world. Racism, colonialism, neocolonialism, imperialism, and other antics of subjugation have pitched the colonizers over the combatants.

Cultural differences have bred suspicion, misunderstanding, and conflict. Differing ideological persuasions, such as Cold War, bred out of the ashes of capitalism and communism, led to tension between the Western and Eastern hemispheres, apart from the arms race and limited wars it generated. Extravagant nationalism and arrogant sovereignty have stimulated wars because of extreme beliefs that had to be expressed in military adventurism or guerrilla tactics.

There are economic conditions which stand as barriers to peace, not only between capitalism and communism but between the North and the South, between the developed and the underdeveloped, and between the have and the have-not nations. The struggle for resource control between the technologically advanced nations of the world and the less technologically third world countries, which have the resources, have continued to engender rivalry and tension, thereby threatening peaceful international coexistence.

Militarism, that is, military coups, military regimes, and the participation of officers in the decision making process of government, where their views and needs are seen as those of the nation state itself, is capable of frustrating peace workers who believe that civil democracy is superior to militocracy. The producers of weapons of destruction are close allies of military adventurists who believe that power must be derived from the barrels of the gun, rather than the bullions of balloting box.

As noted elsewhere, "Those who plan a nation's defense envisage even remote threats, and then make elaborate plans on how to thwart these perceived dangers. Militarism has accelerated the simulation of war games and 'worst possible scenarios."

The result has been "the development of generations of new weapon systems and constantly rising defense budgets." One fundamental obstacle to permanent peace on earth is the very fact that war has been institutionalized by the world, thereby making its eradication near impossible. The saying, "If you want peace, prepare for war," is more of a military jargon than universal adage, canvassed and advanced by war mongers than peace promoters. Yet, peace advocates are the vanguards of freedom, just as war mongers are agents of anarchy and destruction.

The good news is that even though pacifists and peacemakers have faced tremendous obstacles, they, nonetheless, have not despaired; rather they have in numerous ways sought to counteract war and its evil consequences. From the teachings of Jesus Christ on peace and nonviolence, regardless of provocation in the New Testament, to Greek sages, such as Socrates, Plato, Aristotle, and others who had earlier formulated ideas of diplomacy, international law, the resolution of disputes by way of arbitration, to the Roman emperors, who tried the tactics of imposing peace by force as well as their concept of *Pax Romana*, help to promote stability for centuries in Large expanses of their empire. In the fifth century, the great Catholic saint, Augustine, tried to differentiate between "a just and an unjust war" in his desire to set some limit on extensive use of force if war became inevitable.

In this effort, he felt that "if a situation of war was unjust and efforts to resolve issues failed, fighting may be justified." But he was quick to point out that "even then excessive force should not be used, the enemy should be punished only according to the severity of the offense, and peace settlements should avoid harsh terms." As for medieval thinkers and writers, war was out of the question, but when it became inevitable, "congress or leagues [should] be formed to which nations could submit their disputes for settlement."

The French Revolution and the Napoleonic wars gave Europe and the United States a fillip to seek for peace more pragmatically. Thus, in the United States, the first society for peace appeared in 1815 and the second in Britain in 1816. The American Peace Society, which began in 1928, labored for international détente and conciliation apart from sponsoring a number of peace congresses, while the *Ligue internationale et permanent de la paix* in Paris in 1867, and the *Ligue internationale et permanent de la paix et de la liberte* in Geneva the same year. After this, more influential groups sprang up rapidly in Western European countries and the United States until the establishment of the Carnegie Endowment for International Peace in 1910.

But apart from persons and private groups, government also sought to diminish warfare. The Congress of Vienna (1814–1815), helped to stabilize Europe in a number of ways through wide-ranging agreements, which were further reiterated in subsequent conferences, such as the Aix- la-Chapelle (1818), Troppeau and Laibach (1820–1821), and Verona (1822). Later in the nineteenth century, political leaders met in Paris (1856), Berlin (1878 and 1885), Brussels (1890), to resolve outstanding problems in Europe, the Balkans, and Africa. Thereafter, national leaders met often to discuss matters of serious concern. For example, in 1899 in The Hague, delegates from twenty-six governments assembled to discuss armaments, rules of warfare, and arbitration processes. In 1907, representatives from forty-four countries met again in The Hague to investigate similar issues. The birth of Permanent Court of Arbitration in 1898 was their singular achievement, which was born out of discussions in sessions.

In 1919, forty-two states met in Paris where the League of Nations was created, thereby facilitating diplomatic dialogues in interwar years. In 1922, a successful accord was struck on disarmament in the form of Five-Power Washington Naval Treaty. In 1928, the Kellogg-Briand Pact known to history as the "outlawry of war treaty" renounced war as an instrument of national policy and agreed to submit their disputes to peaceful settlement. Unfortunately, all these herculean efforts failed to sustain world peace, with the result that another world war took center stage. But by establishing the United Nations in 1945, governments and world leaders showed a growing commitment to peace efforts rather than war affronts. The creation of the World Bank (1946), the Universal Declaration of Human Rights (1948), the General Agreement on Tariffs and Trades (1948), and the International Atomic Energy Agency (1957) are some of the positive post-World War II agreements amongst nations.

But even though the pace of peace movements was affected by tensions of the Cold War between the United States and the Soviet Union, which created military threats, concerns over nuclear buildup made many people to rally against superpowers arms buildup and delivery systems. There were extensive protest against atmospheric testing and nuclear preparedness, which helped to achieve the

Multilateral Test-Ban convention of 1963, the Outer Space Accord of 1967, the Nonproliferation Treaty of 1968, the Strategic Arms Limitation Talks (SALT), and the Strategic Arms Reduction Talks (START). In the US, many Americans opposed the war with Vietnam where they thought their government was wrong; in doing so, people did not hesitate to employ Gandhian nonviolent tactics, which the dynamic Martin Luther King Jr. had popularized in the New World, to achieve their goals and objectives.

The twentieth century witnessed the arrival of new movements for promoting peace as people directed their energies at creating legal and politically oriented institutions designed to achieve a stable world. These included the Permanent Court of International Justice (1921–1946), and the International Court of Justice established in 1946. They worked to develop and extend the peaceful resolution of conflicts through mediation, conciliation, and arbitration. The League of Nations and the United Nations had their agencies and commissions and committees for the open discussion of international concerns.

The International Labor Organization, World Health Organization, and the Food and Agricultural Organizations remain a heritage of efforts aimed at promoting stability in the world. While the League of Nations and the United Nations have not been able to resolve world conflicts totally, their peacekeeping efforts in trouble spots, such as Kashmir, the Middle East, Greece, Lebanon, Cyprus, the Congo, Rwanda, Burundi, and Somalia should be high-lighted and appreciated.

In addition to international organizations, such as the

League of Nations and the United Nations, the place of regional international organizations such as the Council of Europe, the Organization of American States, the Organization of African Unity (now African Union), and their parallel in the Asian world, sought in their geographical areas to resolve differences that required no world attention. In addition, mention must be made of extensive activity outside political channels to institutionalize international behaviors as thousands of business, labor, intellectual, cultural, scientific, and educational societies, unions, and associations grew. Presently, the focus is on peace research and education. Such institutions as the United States institute of Peace, Canadian Peace Research Institute, Stockholm International Peace Research Institute, the Institute for Peace and Conflict Resolution in Abuja, Nigeria, and similar bodies in other countries are meant to examine issues of war and peace scientifically. By seeking answers to the causes of war, effects of military expenditure, how wars have been, and can be averted, and the history and tactics of peace movements and ideas, they try to explore those aspects of human relations, which tend toward violent behaviors.

In addition, peace education programs in universities and colleges seek to provide insight and understanding on the complexity of war through multidisciplinary study. Here, they hope to inform the educated class on crises and options thereby indirectly influencing decision makers. According to them, change is possible if issues are examined critically and nationally.

From the foregoing historical excursion, it is clear the

efforts of concerned individuals, who have kept the ideal of peace alert, have contributed immensely in keeping our world alive. Even though the world has been suffering from pockets of conflagration in various "axis of evils," the prospects of future peace lies in the hands of those who will, like their predecessors, labor to develop new ideas and options, who will develop processes for the reduction of tensions as well as peaceful resolution of conflicts, and who will create more institutions for the promotion of peace in the world.

The late Reggae legend, Bob Marley, says in one of his evergreen lyrics that:

"Until the philosophy that holds one race superior and another inferior is finally and permanently discredited and abandoned, there will be war. Until then, the dream of lasting peace, world citizenship, and the rule of international morality will remain but a fleeting illusion to be pursued, but never attained."

This advice of Bob Marley is yet to be heeded by mankind.

At the Global Peace and Forgiveness Foundation, we are ever ready to extend our hand of fellowship to all peace promoters in all parts of the world in order to make the world a better place to live.

So help us God!

JUSTICE WITHOUT INJURY

"Though force can protect in emergency, only Justice, fairness, consideration, and cooperation can finally lead men to the down of eternal Peace."

—Dwight D. Esienhower

NO MATTER THE terminologies and vocabularies employed and displayed by verbal disputants and intellectual acrobatics on the eternal question of justice, it is universally acknowledged that there is a difference between right and might, between fairness and foulness, between frankness and falseness, and between utility and expediency. Right from time immemorial, there has been a difference of opinion and conflict of argument between those who believe that might make right, and those who think that right cannot be expended on the altar of expediency.

On the other hand, there are some who reason that justice is mere opportunism, just as there are those who argue that power can be rightly as well as wrongly applied. Still, there are many who point out that justice as measured by men and states cannot be measured as utility.

The sabre-rattlings notwithstanding, the interest of man in justice is ever sustained because of his moral scruples. Since man is a rational and moral being, anything that spikes or offends his conscience must be scrutinized and explained in the light of reason and experience. This is where morality and legality are intertwined with the vexed question of justice. Whereas what is morally pure can be legally upheld, it is not what is legally tenable that can always be morally defended. Yet, the perennial questions of morality and legality are linked with justice because it affects both the strong and the weak.

Even though the ancients believed that "right as the word goes is only in question between equals in power" and that "whereas the stronger do whatever they can, and the weaker suffer whatever they must," yet the principle of justice cannot be defined within the confine of "the interest of the stronger" only lest man becomes a wolf to his fellow man.

The strong have no right whatever to debar the weak from talking about justice, whether they invite the latter to obey their interest or not, just as the weak have the right to stand up to their interests. This conflict of polar opposites can only be resolved amicably when we heed the admonition of Dwight D. Eisenhower, a former president of the United States of

America, who said, "Though force can protect in emergency, only justice, fairness, consideration, and cooperation can finally lead men to the dawn of eternal peace."

If the stronger thinks that because they have right, as far as they have the might, to exact from the weaker whatever serves their interests or that their laws or demands cannot be unjust or that they cannot do injustice, then they stand to be condemned from the reprisals by those whom they have oppressed or injured, as the ancient sages argue.

Now, for purposes of clarity, the definition of justice gives more meaning to our understanding and behavior. According to *Oxford Advanced Learner's Dictionary*, justice means "right and fair behavior or treatment." It also means "the quality of being fair or reasonable." By extension, justice refers to dealing with somebody properly and in an appropriate manner. Therefore, to do justice to somebody or to do somebody justice means to represent the person fairly.

The foregoing elastic definition of justice helps us to understand that whether in law courts or in the courts of public opinion, the concept of justice makes all men equal before the law and the society. It is therefore in the interpretation or misrepresentation of law that injustice creeps into the courts, the society or community.

But to have a clearer picture of this point of view, the opposite of justice, which is injustice, needs to be defined too. Again, let us take our reference from the same dictionary: "Injustice is lack of justice; it is an unfair act; it is an instance of unfair treatment." It is also an "act of judging oneself or somebody else unfairly." From the above definitions, the lack of justice gives room for a negative reaction. Victims of injustice are a sad reminder to us all that the world needs a new rebirth of justice and freedom. Every miscarriage of justice calls for the need to fight injustice. To expose the injustice of any given system is to do the society a world of good. Hence social crusaders, human right activists, freedom fighters, and political emancipators often see themselves as acolytes of redemption.

But it is one thing to suffer injustice. It is quite another thing to perpetrate injustice. Those who perpetrate injustice are worse offenders against humanity, and even the laws of God, as Hosea Ballou opines, "Those who commit injustice bear the greatest burden." They bear the greatest burden because their conscience stands sentinel over their iniquity. They bear the greatest burden because the society knows their misdeed. And they bear the greatest burden because of the Law of Karma or the Law of Compensation or Natural Justice. As the Christian knows, 'whatever a man sows, this shall he also reap."

God is a God of justice. Hence, He demands justice, fair play, and right conduct in human interrelationships. This forms the basis of religious sanity. Indeed, the precept "to render unto others what is their due" suggests that "when the just is conceived as the fair, the fairness which is due to us should also apply to others generally."

The precepts of justice encompass doing good, harming no one, rendering to each his own. It is treating equals equally. As Isaiah, the son of Amoz puts it, "These are the words of the *Lord*: maintain justice, do right, for my deliverance is close at hand, and my righteousness will show itself victorious. Happy is the man who follows these precepts, happy the mortal who holds them fast…who refrains from all wrongdoings (Isaiah 56:1–2)."

In righteousness and justice, mankind is summoned to seek good and not evil, to hate evil and love good, and to enthrone justice in courts of law. Why is justice the organizing principle of an ideal state?

Because, in the words of Aristotle, the son of Aristomachus and Plato's disciple, "Justice is the bond of men in states, for the administration of justice, which is the determination of what is just, is the principle of order in political society." No wonder he described man "as the worst of animals," when separated from law and justice, while St. Augustine paints the state without justice as "no better than a bands of robber thieves."

A government that does not uphold the principle of justice in its administrative ethos, thereby transgresses the natural rights of its citizens and negates its own reason for being in power, since governments are instituted among men to secure their inalienable rights. What the state does not create, can it destroy? How can those who deny natural rights have standards when governments violate the rights and invade the liberties of their citizens? If men are considered to have no rights except those granted by their rulers, absolute power, which the rulers exercise, can only be criticized and condemned as tyrannical and despotic.

No wonder, John Locke observes in "a state of perfect freedom," apart from government and civil institutions that this state of nature "has a law of nature to govern it, which obliges everyone; and reason, which is that law, teaches all mankind who will but consult it that, things being all equal and independent, no one ought to harm another in his life, health, liberty, or provisions." Locke's law of nature implies the principle of just dealing between men, especially when they associate in the common life of a civil society. According to him and other great thinkers of the world, "natural justice and natural rights" remain in existence "to limit the powers of government and to measure the justice of its laws."

From these ancient maxims, we can deduce a few lessons, germane to our world of today. First, without the instrument of justice to bind civilized nations and human beings together, the world will drift into the Hobbesian state of nature: "a condition of war of everyone against everyone," whereby "every man has a right to do everything, even to another's body."

But since this is no ideal state for anyone, the fertile application of justice as "the constant will to render to each man what is his due" smacks of better relevance.

Secondly, justice is a virtue and quality of human acts, hence the divine injunction to seek the good "and to avoid evil." By doing good to others, by injuring no one, and by rendering to every man his own, the concept of justice can be used to further the peace and harmony of a society.

Thirdly, the deduction of Thomas Aquinas that "love is a unitive force" is worthy of universal commendation and observation, while William Shakespeare's declaration of how "earthly power doth then show likest God's when mercy seasons justice" compares favorably with charity, forgiveness, justice, peace, and reconciliation as great attributes under a universal law of freedom.

"Peace is the work of justice," according to Thomas Aquinas, because without justice, there can be no peace. Justice facilitates the routes to peace by removing obstacles to forgiveness and reconciliation. Charity causes peace and maintains harmony. Charity without chaos extends the bonds of friendship, while justice governs their interaction. The generosity of love commands or impels men to live and let live, to give and be given, hence mercy and charity qualify justice as a leavening process in human relationships.

Laws that are based on the principles of justice egg men on to campaign for social Justice. In the words of Aristotle, "The just is the lawful and the fair," for the just man is known by his just acts. Justice makes men to fulfill their obligations for the common good. General justice promotes happiness, for it sows the seeds of peace and other social virtues. Peace with justice is the goal of Global Peace and Forgiveness Foundation.

The law of the jungle or the principle of lex talionis—an eye for an eye, a tooth for a tooth, a life for a life—are primitive and negative aspects of justice, while injustice constitutes an injury to others and thereby despoils the society.

Yes, domestic justice examines the problems of right and duty in the family; economic justice looks at justice in production, distribution, and exchange; political justice addresses the question of justice in government, while legal justice confers equity in the application of human law.

Yet, we can only agree with that ancient visionary, Socrates, the Greek sage, that "it is better to suffer than to do injustice," because "the man who is wronged suffers injury in body or external things, while the man who does wrong injures his own soul by destroying its greatest good." The challenge of the hour is to promote justice without injury to our souls.

FORGIVENESS WITHOUT FRICTION

"To err is human; to forgive, divine."
—Alexander Pope

WHEN HENRY WARD Beecher, the famous orator, clergyman, and abolitionist was writing on the importance of forgiveness, he said, "'I can forgive, but I cannot forget' is only another way of saying, 'I will not forgive.' Forgiveness ought to be like a canceled note torn in two and burned up so that it never can be shown against one." To him, forgiveness is synonymous with forgetfulness. In other words, forgiveness should be total to be meaningful to the forgiven.

According to Jean and Richter, "Humanity is never so beautiful as when praying for forgiveness or else forgiving another." In the views of these noble writers, human beings are favored in the sight of God whenever they pray for forgiveness, because God is a forgiver! But they did not stop there; they also pointed out that there is nobility in the hearts of those who forgive others. They believed rightly that to be forgiven, we must learn to forgive our kind, no matter the gravity of provocation.

Forgiveness is not a sign of weakness. Far from it. In fact, forgiveness is a mark of strength in the sight of God. Otherwise, Jesus Christ would not have forgiven the good thief on the cross; he also would not have asked God to forgive those who ridiculed and nailed him to the cross. By asking God to forgive his killers, Jesus of Nazareth demonstrated the dignity of divinity to humanity.

When the great Indian nationalist and patriot, Mahatma Gandhi, was challenging the British colonial curtain over India, he was made an object of public ridicule. Not only by the colonizers, but by some Indians who felt more at home with the yoke of colonialism than freedom from servitude. But, he did not hold their weaknesses against them. Rather he said, "The weak can never forgive. Forgiveness is the attribute of the strong." Mahatma Gandhi had the milk of human kindness in his breasts, and he forgave all those who revolted against him or against his nonviolent resistance movement, because he knew the power of forgiveness over his foes.

Forgiveness is the ability or willingness to stop being angry or bitter toward somebody over a perceived or actual wrong. It is the willingness to stop blaming or wanting to punish somebody because of a wrong suffered. Forgiveness is the readiness to forget about a wrong suffered.

Friendship thrives on forgiveness because friends are always ready to forgive and forget their lapses against each other. Nobody can keep a true friend for long who does not know how to forgive and forget the shortcomings of his friend. The ability to forgive and forget is a mark of genuine friendship and bonds of stability, as demonstrated by David and Jonathan—two great friends.

Those who show love and forgiveness to their enemies are friends of God. "And be ye kind one to another, tender hearted, forgiving one another, even as God for Christ's sake hath forgiven you (Ephesians 4:32)."

This is the word of God, according to the Christian Holy Bible, asking man to be kind to one another, tender- hearted, and forgiving, even as God forgives man.

Most religion preaches forgiveness, and every man desire to be forgiven his sins, mistakes, or shortcomings.

Man, desires to be forgiven his wrongs, even when he is guilty. This is the nature of man. It is also the nature of God to forgive that is why the Holy Bible advises man to forgive his kind and be tender-hearted.

Where there is tender heart, there is forgiveness. The need for forgiveness cannot be over emphasized, for it is the major ingredient for pure heart—a heart devoid of offense toward others.

If forgiveness must be total, both the wrong and the wronged owe it as a duty to forgive and forget the cause of disagreement, if they are ever to know the peace that wells up from forgiveness.

Both parties should be ready to forget the past, and if possible, no reference should be made to the incident. There should be no victor, no vanquished between those who forgive and those who accept forgiveness.

Forgiveness is the panacea for peace. Without forgiveness, there will be no peace, whether in the family unit or national entity.

Lack of forgiveness has caused a lot of destruction to mankind. It has bred enmity. It has been the cause of wars of nations fighting nations, of tribes fighting tribes, of families fighting families, and even of individuals fighting individuals. The lack of forgiveness is also the cause of human underdevelopment. Where there is no forgiveness, there is underdevelopment since it brings disagreement among neighbors—which affects their environment—their neighborhood, state, or nation.

Whatsoever is the cause for disagreement, there should be room for forgiveness, which will naturally lead to reconciliation. Right from when God created the world, man has always disagreed with his fellowman, and this has led to bad blood, and sometimes, dire consequences for mankind.

There is need for forgiveness, and when forgiving, every other consideration should be put aside by us to make it real. If possible, there should be no conditions attached to forgiveness. It must be total and unconditional.

It has been observed that when people claim to have forgiven one another, they still allow causes of the disagreement to rear its ugly head again, which causes new hatred and other ungodly actions among them. But if forgiveness should be permanent, it should be without preconditions.

The *Oxford Advanced Learner's Dictionary* describes friction as disagreement or conflict between people or parties with different views. This definition clearly states that disagreement or conflict among people or parties leads to friction, and ultimately to trouble and unforgiveness.

But if forgiveness should be without friction, then all areas of disagreements should be honestly tabled, discussed, and settled to the satisfaction of both parties. Forgiveness without friction is total.

Friction leads to recurrence of past disagreement with dire consequences including riots, killings, religious uprisings, and social upheavals. But if peace is to reign without conflict, we should trash out issues with all honesty and look out for genuine ways of seeking lasting solutions to them.

There is no problem without solution. Even the most complex problems have been solved by man. All man needs are the will to succeed.

The world has fought two world wars and countless numbers of other lesser wars, and after extensive losses of lives and destruction of properties, agreements for peace have been reached and normalcy restored due to the spirit of forgiveness displayed both by the victor and vanquished. Yet, the belligerents later became the best of friends. This is true of USA, Britain, Germany, Japan, and Russia, and others in world history.

However, we look at it, the need for forgiveness among

people is real. Any society where there is no forgiveness, peace, development, prosperity, and other positive elements will vanish through the back door.

Bitterness, which is the seed of unforgiveness, has stood against the development of man and nations. Unresolved crises or partially resolved conflicts lead to bitterness due to unsatisfied positions of the combatants. It then becomes peace of the grave type of existence amongst people.

Because of the need for 'peaceful coexistence,' any slight provocation by either party that can lead to fresh hostilities should be nipped in the bud before it causes more trouble for mankind. This especially needed in countries, such as Nigeria, where ethnic and religious rivalries always snow-ball into giant conflicts.

Unforgiveness and bitterness stemming from age-long grievances are the major causes of these renewed conflicts.

Unless and until the people, including their leaders, are willing to genuinely seek real peace by forgiving perceived wrongs, the world will continue to reel from one crisis to another.

History testifies to the fact that where people do not forgive and put the past wrongs behind them, peace is never their portion, for such people will always live in fear, uncertainty, and mutual suspicion.

What then does it profit an individual or a nation not to forgive? It does not profit any man to strive in unforgiveness or bitterness against his neighbor.

Unforgiveness and bitterness bring isolation and dejection to men and their nations. On the other hand, nations that have had conflicts or disagreements and have settled their differences, are enjoying peace and development today. (e.g., Vichy France reconciled with Free French during the Second World War, under Marshal Petain and General Charles de Gaulle. Ditto the former two Germans and other nations with similar experiences,). People and nations need to critically look into the issue of settling their differences with the aim of analyzing the causes of constant friction between them and seeking ways for permanent settlement. When nations refuse to accept forgiveness, they remain fragmented, or they disintegrate, such as Yugoslavia and Czechoslovakia, now sadly reminds us.

There is no doubt that forgiveness, which removes friction, brings peace, and peace in turn brings development with its advantages. It pays everyone to live in peace because peace also breeds a settled and organized society. This can only be achieved through forgiveness.

The need for individuals and nations to try and forgive themselves of whatsoever offenses—past or present—allegedly committed by their fore bearers or even their own generation should be paramount. Any cause of disagreement should be buried in the dust bin of history; instead, issues that will promote the corporate existence of individuals or communities should take center stage. Issues that will bring back sad memories of past disagreements should be discouraged by all and sundry.

Most importantly, whatsoever is the belief of man, be it secular or spiritual, none encourages him to live a life of friction, which is the harbinger of unforgiveness. Sound doctrines, be they of God or man, promote peace, wealth, prosperity, good health, long life, development, and other good things of life, for real peace can only be possible through forgiveness without friction.

RECONCILIATION WITHOUT REGRETS

"if we ever forget that we are One Nation Under God, then we will be a nation gone under"

—Ronald Reagan

IN WRITING THIS book, the Global Peace and Forgiveness Foundation is very conversant with the conflicts afflicting various part of the world today. As a matter of fact, it will amount to intellectual delusion to assume that the world as presently constituted can live permanently in peace, without any form of strife, conflict, or war. But at the same time, most of the conflict, strifes, and wars can always be resolved at the roundtable. That is where reconciliation comes in.

The art of reconciliation can always be facilitated by common apology. People can become friends again after a quarrel, no matter how bitter. Divorced couples are known to have remarried after reconciliation. Prodigal children, disowned by their parents, have been known to return home to a loving family embrace. After conflict resolution, warring nations have been known to lay down their weapons of war. So, there is always room for reconciliation without regrets and war without weapons.

The need for reconciliation among men is vital to human progress because of its centrality to development and peaceful coexistence. Reconciliation can only be achieved if men are ready to forgive one another their shortcomings, mistakes, and weaknesses.

For man or nation to enjoy peace and development, all areas of disagreement between his fellow men or its different components, be it individual or group, derived therefore. History has proved beyond reasonable doubt that reconciliation of peoples and nations has benefitted mankind rather than allowing irreconcilable differences to fester. Nations have gone to war to solve problems with their perceived enemies, and whether they win the war or not, they have always resorted to the roundtable, where reconciliation is sought and attained.

Reconciliation is an end to disagreements, and when it is sought, it should be without prejudice.

The good book, the *Holy Bible*, encourages man to seek reconciliation with his fellow man when it says, "Follow peace with all men and holiness without which no man shall see God.'' It further encourages man to leave whatsoever he is doing, even when offering sacrifice to God, and go and reconcile with his fellow man before coming back to offer his sacrifice to God before it can be acceptable. These references illustrate to us the importance which God attaches to forgiveness and reconciliation.

God who is the Creator of man encourages and approves reconciliation among men. He even insists that it is a condition which man must fulfill before he can see him (or reach heaven).

Most religions and beliefs also encourage adherents to embrace reconciliation as part of conflict resolution by attaching rewards to it. For example, Islam encourages its followers to live in peace with non-Muslims and seek peace and reconciliation with their neighbors. Christianity, on the other hand, commands all believers to love their neighbors as they love themselves.

In the old times, before the coming of modern civilization to Africa, when Africa was predominantly made up of traditional ethnic groups, reconciliation was an effective and cost-saving measure of resolving conflicts, and it was applied at every level of resolving them. This method was applied at the individual, group, national, and transnational levels with good results.

Thus, at whatever level there is a conflict, and however small or large the problem may be, the most profitable method to adopt in resolving such a matter was through reconciliation—be it among friends or foe, be it among members of the same family or clan, be it among tribes or nation, be it among people of the same country or different countries, reconciliation, as a form of conflict resolution, has never failed to provide the needed result.

Reconciliation has been described as the butter of life. It is the lubricant that oils the process for which peace is attained through understanding, perseverance, love, and forgiveness. No wonder reconciliation has been ordained by God to enable mankind to sort themselves out peacefully.

In the Holy Books, evidences abound where reconciliation has been encouraged and attained by formerly sworn enemies, and such actions were approved by God. For example, the Bible tells us of the reign of King David of Israel and the peace he had roundabout him during his tenure. The Bible tells that all the kings and kingdoms about Israel were at peace with Israel. It was not so before his reign, for Israel was at war with all its neighbors. This peaceful coexistence with Israel's neighbors then was achieved through the reconciliatory efforts of King David, who valued peace as a divine blessing.

In African tradition, reconciliation is a useful instrument in conflict resolution. Whenever there is a disagreement between parties, arrangements are made to resolve the matter, and this is usually done at a "Peace Hall," where traditional delicacies like kola nuts, alligator pepper, food, and wine are brought by one or both parties as a sign of forgiveness or brotherliness and in the spirit of reconciliation. In this atmosphere, even the most difficult problems are amicably settled to the satisfaction of both parties.

Whatever the type and nature of the conflict is, this method has always been successful in resolving African problems.

During the partition of Africa, despite the aggressive

nature of the colonial adventurers and the destruction of lives and properties of the natives and the evils that went along with colonization, including slavery, Africans still decided to forgive their conquerors and tormentors because of the spirit of reconciliation imbued in the African way of life.

Today, Africa and their former colonial masters are the best of friends, engaging in productive activities, such as diplomacy, trade, and commerce, despite the atrocities meted out to them by the colonial mercenaries. Wars have been fought, lost, and won. Loss of lives and destruction of properties have taken place since the creation of the world. Untold calamities caused by man have befallen men.

The future of men and nations has been wiped off the map of the world through conflicts and none has been the better for it. Multifarious class and colonial wars have been fought. The First and Second World Wars were also fought. Political, ideological, religious, and sectional wars have been fought to settle real or perceived differences, but all efforts at resolving issues with force have been in vain with no positive results.

The First and Second World Wars gave birth to the League of Nations in 1919 and the United Nations in 1945. These international organizations were made possible through dialogue and the quest for peace through reconciliation.

Even in the turbulent period of the Cuban Missile crisis in 1962, dialogue and reconciliation proved once again that there is no better alternative to conflict resolution when the conflicting nations realized that despite their world power status, all their arsenal should have led the world to war, massive destruction, and possible elimination of mankind from the face of the earth.

Before this time, however, major wars, such as the Napoleonic wars and the American Civil War, were finally resolved through dialogue and reconciliation. The Nigerian Civil War was no exception. It lasted three years with over three million lives lost and properties worth billions of dollars destroyed. At the end of it all, combatants on both sides of this conflicts agreed that there was no victor, no vanquished. The spirit of reconciliation was thus once again proved to be the best antidote to the fraternal slaughter.

The list of those individuals, groups, nations and even the international organizations that had, at one time or the other, embraced reconciliation as a policy for conflict resolution have endured to savor such moments. Reconciliation has brought back peace, development, and stability to continents, countries, and communities.

Let us go down memory lane and see those individuals who failed to toe the line of dialogue and reconciliation and what was the result of their action or inaction. These examples will assist in exposing us to the dangers of rejecting dialogue and reconciliation as a weapon for settlement of conflicts and its attendant disadvantages.

When King Shaka, the Zulu, a great African king, refused to dialogue and sought reconciliation with his neighbors and invading colonialists, his empire was destroyed, and he lost his life in the process.

When the war mongers Adolf Hitler, Benito Benito Mussolini of Italy, fascists alike toed the part of war and destruction, and refused to seek peace despite all the opportunities they had to write their names in gold as men who would have brought the Second World War to an end, they ended up writing their names in blood and in the mud as they were eventually consumed by the fire they ignited. While Adolf Hitler committed suicide, Benito Mussolini was captured and killed ignominiously by Italian partisan fighters.

The UNITA (National Union of the Total Independent of Angola) rebel, Jonas Savimbi of Angola and Slobodan Milosevic, former president of Yugoslavia, were another set of men history gave an opportunity to put their names in the world's hall of fame. If only they had embraced dialogue and reconciliation in resolving the conflicts in their countries, if only they had not allowed the monster of war and destruction to overwhelm them, they would not have been condemned and consumed accordingly—one by death in the battlefield and the other by the International Wars Crimes Tribunal in the Hague. In countries, such as Nigeria and Sudan, where ethnic and religious conflicts have become pervasive and recurrent, one adducible reason can be traced to stubborn resistance by community leaders and religious zealots who are usually against the finer principles of dialogue and reconciliation as the means to resolve their differences.

The elements of hypocrisy and deceit that such leaders often exhibit, often betrays the collective resolve to live in peace rather than pieces. Their differences will not achieve the desired results but will lead to escalation of the problems.

In looking for conflict resolutions, parties to conflicts should seek reconciliation with pure heart, devoid of offense, and with the intention to forgive and forget the cause of conflict or disagreement. The ability to forgive and forget is a divine attribute.

There are no half measures in seeking reconciliation. It is either both parties are ready to make amends and reconcile or they are at war without peace. But in the cause of reconciliation, parties involved should be honest to themselves and every likely cause for disagreements should be made known as lasting solutions are found for them. The ways and means of avoiding mistakes of the past and machinery to resolve future conflicts should be put in place.

Both sides should be ready to accept faults and make amends and accept the verdict of the arbitration efforts they were part of. This is the surest way for conflicting parties to work out reconciliation without regrets. If there is reconciliation among the contending people of the world, the world shall live in peace, harmony, and concord, thereby facilitating a new world order.

PRAYER WITHOUT PRESSURE

"When one feels discouraged, a prayer will rekindle his courage and ambition; when one feels sick, a prayer will serve as the best tonic; when one feels that all the world is against him, a prayer will bring new life, joy, happiness, and a better understanding to his soul! A prayer for others is the greatest prayer ever uttered, and surely, such unselfish supplication cannot fail to reach the ear of deity and be rewarded with answer on its echo wave."

—J. W. Dickson

BEFORE SIR ISAAC Newton, the great European scientist alerted the world with the new Law of Gravity, he was engrossed in telescoping the universe. But more than that, he saw the importance of prayer, which he utilized for the benefits of the world. To appreciate his thoughts at that material time, let us see what he put in black and white: "I can take my telescope and look millions and millions of miles into space, watch the blazing sun and rolling planets in the infinite depths of immensity, but I can lay it aside and go into my room, shut the door, get down on my knees in earnest prayer, and see more of heaven, and get closer to God through His word than I can be assisted by all the telescopes and materials agencies of earth." Thus, Sir Isaac Newton prayed without pressure.

When Professor S. F. B. Morse was laboring in the vineyards of a university in order to bless the world with the telegraph, he did not rely on grey matter in his head alone. Rather, he found insight for his invention—through prayer. Fortunately, he left his testimony in the following words: "Many a time when I was making my experiments in my laboratory in the university, I would come to a standstill, not knowing what to do next. An obstacle would present itself that seemed to be insurmountable. A mental fog would cloud my mind that would not clear away.

"But, during such times, I always locked my doors, knelt down and prayed for light and help. And light and help invariably came." Thus, like Sir Isaac Newton, Morse prayed without pressure.

What of Lord Kelvin, one of the greatest scientists of the nineteenth century? Did he pray in his scientific research? You bet he did! And for the generations, he left a record. Let us see what he has to say: "Every discovery I have made that has contributed to the benefit of man he (God) has given me in answer to prayer." Thus, like Newton and Morse, Lord Kelvin prayed.

From the foregoing records, we do know that scientists, who matter, do pray. If in doubt, ask the Wizard of Menlo Park, Thomas Alva Edison! If in doubt, ask Albert Einstein, the Atom Archer! If in doubt, ask other leading lights in scientific discovery and invention. The question therefore is this: if scientists could pray without pressure, what about you? What about me?

Religion enjoins man to pray and communicate with his Creator. That is why Jesus Christ, the founder and shepherd of Christianity, prayed before, during, and after his ministry. That is why the Bible commands Christians to pray without ceasing. That is why Prophet Mohammed prayed five times a day and left a legacy for Muslims to follow. That is why Hindus, Buddhists, Zoroastrians, Taoists, Hare Krishna's, and even Traditional Religious worshippers pray for higher understanding in their affairs.

Prayer without pressure is the ability to pray without being prompted. It is the capacity to pray without ceasing. It is the readiness to pray for world peace. It is the willingness to pray for forgiveness where there is friction. It is the desire to pray for religion without riots. It is the interest to pray for reconciliation without regrets. It is the endeavor to pray for justice without injury. It is the concern to pray for others as we would like them to pray for us.

Prayer without pressure is altruistic because it emphasizes the interests of others, as much as our own. It is the confession of the soul before a merciful Father. It is the request from the Most High that there be peace on earth and goodwill toward others. It is the kind of supplication, which looks for answer from the Creator. It is also an expression of thanks for all that the good God has done, and which He will yet do for His earthly siblings.

Prayer without pressure is the most appealing form of supplication known to mankind, for it is the soul-satisfying language uttered by both the rich and the poor. It is asking earnestly for what is desired, which only God can do.

Prayer without pressure looks forwards for the good, the true, and the beautiful. It looks for the good in God; it looks for the truth in Man; it looks for the beautiful in the world. It accords with the Sermon on the Mount, *blessed are the prayerful, for they shall be compensated.*

Prayer without pressure recognizes the fact that God answers prayer. "Ask and ye shall receive." It knows that the affairs of the world cry for divine intervention. It solicits heavenly solutions to earthly problems. It yearns for security with safe borders. It cries for peace, forgiveness, and reconciliation, where there is panic, misunderstanding, and injustice. It acts as a catalyst for human redemption.

The goodness of God, the hope of man, and the joy of eternity all make a good case for prayer without pressure. The urgent need for peace with justice and forgiveness with reconciliation gives a hand of fellowship to prayer without pressure. Prayer is a natural spiritual reaction to the need for peace, forgiveness, and reconciliation, without being prompted to do so. Prayer offers mankind the unique opportunity to commune with God for his blessings, and bounties on the world.

But what is prayer? As a definition, prayer is a solemn request or expression of thanks; it may either be to God or an object of worship. It is man's effort to commune with his creator or higher power. Man does not pray to himself. He prays to a superior authority. In most cases a deity or God. When man prays, he prays for himself or others. We may not know how prayer entered the universe, but it is safe to say that the origin of prayer is as old as mankind, for Adam was known to "talk to God" in the Garden of Eden. Since then, man has always believed in a superior being, which he attributes his existence to, and the major means of communicating with this being through prayer.

Prayer can be done in different ways. It can be done quietly or loudly; it can also be done in private or in public. It can be done by one man or a group. It can be done alone or with rituals, such as fasting. Take your pick. The choice is yours or by the dictates of the prayer method you desire.

Man's belief in the efficacy of prayer gives him the confidence to pray. He believes that what cannot be achieved ordinarily can be made possible through prayer.

Just as the song writer says, there are three major reasons man deems it necessary to pray. It is good to pray; in times of difficulty, prayer is the antidote; when man is victorious, prayer is still his method to express his joy and gratitude. The effect of prayer in life of man is enormous, and it has a lasting value.

Prayer is totally the affair of the believer. How a man chooses to pray should be his personal affair and how he decides to pray should be his own business.

There are many religions in the world today, and they all have different ways and methods of communicating with their objects of worship.

Some religious followers claim to pray to the same God but communicate with him in different ways, while even adherents of the same faith have different ways of speaking or reaching their divinity.

Prayer is the means by which man reaches the Supreme Being, in which he believes. This means is developed to suit his way of life and belief. In most cases, he disagrees with the methods of other people in praying to their deity or the same God. He believes that his own method is the best and most effective. Whether to pray is good or not, it has been testified by adherents of different faiths that prayer affects life positively.

Some people provide evidences to show the efficacy of prayer. Governments have also called on their citizens to organize prayer meetings for supernatural intervention in the affairs of state. Even the developed countries of the world are not left out of such prayer calls! In some cases, millions of dollars are spent on organizing prayer meetings and prayer warriors invited to intercede on their behalf for blessings or to forestall national calamities. In other cases, national fasting(s) and prayer(s) with supplication to God have been organized by governments, while some countries still have national prayer days. Groups and organizations, including profit-making companies, are not left out in quest for prayer!

The medium of prayer is so powerful and has a huge influence in the life of man that those who claim to be nonreligious, still desire to be prayed for. It is said that even the devil recognizes the efficacy of prayer!

Prayer therefore is a significant aspect in the life of man, and man should treat it with all seriousness. There was a story of a ship on the high seas, carrying some nationals from different countries on a voyage. Each of them had different religious beliefs. Among them were Christians, Muslims, Hindus, Buddhists, and Taoists.

The take-off journey from port was smooth, until they were on the high seas. A violent storm took over and the ship was in trouble.

Everyone remembered his God and started praying in his own manner. Some were praying silently, while some were praying as loudly as the wicked storm that had befallen the ship. Some even brought out their prayer magic wands and other voodoo materials to invoke divine intervention. In all the ensuing confusion, there was a passenger who was least affected. He was busy sleeping when all the com- motion was going on. When the other passengers found their sleeping companion, they were enraged and lifted him and threw him overboard, accusing him of not having a god to pray to. This simple story illustrates the importance of prayer to man. When praying, a man gives his total being to it. He even sacrifices his time and money and anything that he feels can make his prayer more effective. He sometimes solicits the services of others to pray for him. In Nigeria, there are all kinds of prayer howlers, screaming for their attention and patronage.

Due to the different religious beliefs, patterns of prayer, where and when they are offered, varies in accordance with different beliefs.

Prayers are made in different places of worship, including churches, mosques, public places, or private homes. Prayer can also be said on the streets or inside vehicles. In fact, prayer can be made just anyway and at any time.

Prayer, in one form or the other, is allowed in most countries of the world, because of its universal importance. Certain religions have been banned in different countries of the world, but prayer has never been banned outright anywhere in particular, because human beings run government and all human beings, so-called atheists apart, believe in celestial beings to whom they revert for divine guidance or direction.

Governments have passed legislation in support of prayers directly or indirectly. For example, in Nigeria, there is freedom of religion and worship, freedom of movement, and freedom of speech; freedom of association is entrenched in the constitution. This privilege gives room for citizens—poor or rich—to pray to their God without fear or favor. It also gives them the right to establish their places of worship and prayer, and to promote and propagate their faith without undue harassment.

Some states may legislate on state religions, yet their citizens still have the right to pray either as individuals or groups. As far as prayer is concerned, it does not matter whether a state is secular or religious, communist or capitalist, socialist or welfarist. This also gives the citizens the right to pray to their God the way they deem fit.

One major area where governments should guard against is the misuse of religious privileges. For instance, where adherents of a religion pray to their God, it should not constitute any element of intimidation or harassment to other citizens. It should be done in a way that it will not be a source of embarrassment to others. It should be carried out in the spirit of prayer, which is sacred. It can be stated that due to recognition of religion and prayer, by both man and his government, there is no overemphasizing the fact that prayer is a sacred duty. It is a personal affair between man and his God. For this reason, the right to religious worship and prayer should be respected whether one believes in a creed or not. Every individual should be allowed to pray anyhow, wherever and whenever he desires if it is not against the laws of the land.

Discriminating legislation against religious methods of worship should be discouraged by all governments of the world. Only legislation that encourages people to embrace God ought to be enacted.

Citizens should be encouraged to tolerate the prayer methods of other citizens. There should be no rancor among people in matters of prayer.

Man does not approve or answer prayers, only God does. So, it is not the duty of man or government to determine the method or channels through which people pray to God. Every man should, therefore, be left alone to communicate with God the way he knows best. As a songwriter puts it, "It's a fine thing to pray; prayer is the thing that helps us along when we are weary. That helps us along when we carry a heavy load. Prayer is the thing that makes us happy."

Seeing that prayer is communion with God, realizing that prayer is our soul's desire for God, knowing that "the prayer of a righteous man availeth much"; understanding that without prayer, it is impossible to reach God, and confessing that "men ought always to pray," the Global Peace and Forgiveness Foundation supports all prayer organizations worldwide by praying along with them for world peace geared at forgiveness and universal brotherhood.

We believe that all citizens of the world are patriots of their home countries, for which they should pray fervently. We see that the more we pray, the more evil is averted. The more we pray, the more good is delivered. We remember that God enjoins both individual and collective prayers, just as he welcomes private and public prayers for the good of humanity.

The power of prayer can be demonstrated in this: no matter how difficult or impossible a situation may appear, there is a way out; that way is the way of prayer. As an anonymous writer says,

> Moses prayed; his prayer did save a nation from death and from the grave.
> Joshua prayed. The sun stood still his enemies fell in vale and hill.
> Hannah prayed. God gave her a son; a nation back to

the Lord he won.
Solomon prayed for wisdom then God made him the wisest of mortal men.
Elijah prayed with great desire.
God gave him rain and sent the fire.
Jonah prayed; God heard his wail.
He quickly delivered him from whale.
Three Hebrews prayed, through the flames, they had as a comrade the Son of God.
Elisha prayed with strong emotion; he got the mantle and a double portion.
Daniel prayed; the lions claws were held by angels who locked their jaws.
The lepers prayed, to the priests were sent glory To God! They were healed as they went!
Peter prayed and Dorcas arose to life again, from death's repose.
The thief who prayed for mercy cried he went with Christ to paradise.
The church, she prayed, then got a shock when Peters answered her prayer with a knock!
The disciples kept praying, the spirit came with "cloven tongue" and revival flame!
Conviction filled the heart of men; three thousand souls were "born again" When living faith, for souls imply.
In one accord, united stand— revival fires shall sweep the land! And sinners shall converted be, and all the

world God's glory see!

The lives of Abraham, Moses, Isaiah, Daniel, David, Elijah, Solomon, and Jonah are eternal testimonials to answered prayers. Abraham exemplified a prayerful life by pleading for Sodom and Gomorrah. Moses supplicated for assistance in delivering Israel from the hands of Pharaoh. David consulted God before he ever went to any battle whether personal or national.

Daniel, the pious sage, who served in the kingdom of Babylonia, Media, and Persia, was delivered from the mouth of lions because of his "effectual, fervent prayers." Likewise, King Solomon, the son of David, prayed for wisdom and received riches, honor, and long life as answers from God. Thus, when God answers prayers, he does so with multiple effects.

Indeed, we all have a duty to pray without pressure for ourselves, for our neighbors, for our nations, and for the world, for "it is a fine thing to pray," even as the song writer affirms.

RELIGION WITHOUT RIOTS

"Religion is a subject on which I have ever been most scrupulously reserved. I have considered it as a matter between every man and his maker, in which no other, and far less public, had a right to intermeddle."

—Thomas Jefferson

THE MODERN ASSAULT on religion started with the publication of Charles Darwin's book, The Descent of Man, in 1871, in which he had summed up the firm conclusion of his study by marshalling evidence that man is related to all animal life in the following words:

> "The greatest principle of evolution stands up clear and firm, when these groups of facts are considered in connection with others, such as the mutual affinities of the members of the same group, their geographical distribution in past and present times and their geological succession. It is incredible that all these facts should speak falsely. He who is not content to look, like a savage, at the phenomena of nature as disconnected, cannot any longer believed that man is the work of a separate act of creation."

His finding and writing ignited the ultimate clash between the new biology and theology. His study taught the impersonal process of natural selection as against the inheritance of characteristics, which had been acquired by deliberate efforts. Yet Darwin's struggle for survival and Karl Marx's "survival of the fittest" theories have not succeeded in alienating man from the Creator. Rather, man believed and still believes that beyond his ken of imagination, there is a Supreme Being, a higher intelligence, a greater consciousness, a creative genius, and superstar, who created and controls the universe and all within it.

Indeed, apart from the comparative study of religions, which suggest certain relativity in validity of religious beliefs and rites, the investigation of human biology, physiology, psychology, and sociology and even philosophy have since questioned Darwin's claim to natural selection, while theology reaffirms its traditional belief on creation.

Before Christ's and even Darwin's birth and emergence, religion had always interested mankind. From the Assyrians, to Babylonians, to the code of Hammurabi, to Egyptians, to Grecians, to Romans, and to Africans, the idea of God has registered in human consciousness "not in a philosophical contemplation of God as pure being, pure reason, the highest will, the supreme power, the absolute, but in a study of his perfections, which all have a more or less bearing on men." In the same light, "the immutability of God as standing outside the sphere of changeable things as 'incorruptible,' 'immortal.' The continued existences of the universe, men's safety in dangers are related to God's unchangeableness. The immensity of God is vouchsafed in his other attributes of unity, simplicity, eternity, ubiquity, infinity, and activity."

His divine intellect, divine will, and divine power account for the unoriginated existence in which lies the source of all other originated life. Since man was created in the image of God, man has some of the attributes of God, but in lower cadres. God's goodness, grace, intelligence, wisdom, love, and power are far above man. Since man disserved his affinity with the divinity of God, he needs God to guide him in his earthly pilgrimage. To seek for God's guidance, man turns to religion, amidst its different expressions and interpretations.

"Religion is the opium for the poor." This solemn statement summarizes the opinion of Karl Marx on religion, the eighteenth century Marxist revolutionary, who insisted that the whole world would become one society based on the tenets of communism where everything, including power, will be in the hands of the proletariat. Religion is indeed not the opium of only the poor, but by his extension, of the people, according to him.

There is no doubt that every man believes in one supreme entity or the other, whether visibly seen or otherwise, and looks up to it for supernatural intervention. Man even goes beyond ordinary seeking for protection and provisions from these entities. Because of man's belief of the existence of these entities, his life radiates around them and he is ready to do anything that will please them. Man is ready to challenge any other entity that claims the same or higher authority over his God.

This he does through religious or physical attack on the rival entity or its adherents. Religion is the belief in the existence of God or gods, or a system of faith and worship. It has a controlling influence on the life of its adherents. Its influence on its adherents is indeed intoxicating like opium, and, in most cases, can be compromised for anything else.

Religion is supposed to be a source of blessings to man. In fact, religions have been patterned to be sources of fulfillment and upliftment in human experience. For example, the Islamic faith professes that Islam means peace, while the Christian faith eulogizes Jesus Christ as the Prince of peace.

Religion goes further to encourage and to some extent, instruct, or command its adherents to be of good behavior, to love their fellow men, to be humble and full of generosity, to be forgiving, to respect and honor elders, not to kill a fellow human being, not to steal or destroy the property of one another, and above all, to live a righteous life, and to be rewarded with eternal life.

Doctrines of religion promises reward for faithfulness here on earth and the hereafter.

Religion is indeed one of man's greatest possessions and one of the greatest things that has happened to man. It makes man a disciplined and higher being, quite different from other mammals.

Religion is as old as mankind, and man has been practicing it since his creation. He has always believed in one entity or the other whether he is educated or not, most men hold strongly to a religious belief.

Religion is good for man. In an environment where religion thrives, and its adherents faithfully abide by its instructions, peace, growth, development, and progress are reaped as rewards.

Even where there are adherents of different religions in such communities, these advantages will still be there because every religion preaches and encourages tolerance of other people beliefs and the need for peaceful coexistence.

In truth, most religions insist that the creation of man and total sum is to serve God, therefore, the importance of religion and its role in man's life cannot be thrown to the winds.

Man is supposed to be obedient and faithful to the tenets of his religion. He is expected to surrender all his being to his creator and do everything he has been instructed to do by his God without compromising them.

Then, he will enjoy the rewards for obedience rather than the horrible consequences for disobedience. (Religion offers good moral values, and man's duty as a religious being is to do well and to serve God.)

Unfortunately, religion has become man's greatest albatross. But his problems are not necessarily caused by the doctrines of his religion since most religions preach the good side of life. Instead of man enjoying the good things that come with religion, he has allowed religion to be a pain in the neck.

Because of man's fanaticism for belief and his fear of domination of other religions and the hatred for another man's belief, some religions have become sources of disagreements and conflicts in different areas. Suspicion and rivalry have also reigned supreme, wherever followers of different religions gather, especially in multi-religious societies. These problems have been existing since man embraced religion as a way of life.

History has proved that, from early times, man has been fighting his fellow man over religion. The purpose for such behavior is man's intention to propagate, promote, defend, or extend his religious belief. It is also man's desire to dominate his environment through religion. These acts have led to destruction of lives and properties wherever they occur.

Early man fought tirelessly to propagate or defend his religious beliefs. Empires and kingdoms were destroyed because of the quest for religious supremacy. The Holy Bible and the Noble Qur'an talk of several wars fought in respect of religion, and even quote God as giving approval for some of these wars.

That man has not rested from fighting *one another over religion, is evidenced* in our contemporary times when man is still fighting his fellow man over religion.

Countries or groups of countries are fighting and forming alliances to fight other countries along religious lines, for example, the Arabs versus Israel and their western backers, the Hindus in India, and the Muslims in Pakistan. Also, religious observers of the same faith are forming alliances beyond territorial boundaries to fight perceived enemies, such as can be seen between Muslims and Christians, Hindus and Muslims, in different countries.

Even individuals and groups in the same country also fight themselves because of religious rivalry. Indonesia, Nigeria, and India are leading examples. Some governments are not left out of the battle for religious domination or emancipation. Of these, Saudi Arabia, Iran, Sudan, Algeria, and Iraq qualify.

Some countries have gone to the level of declaring state religions. These include Saudi Arabia, Iran, and Sudan, while others encourage religion based on political parties, such as the Christian Democratic Party in Germany.

Furthermore, the constitution of some countries also encourages the devotion of religious practices. Libya and Afghanistan readily come to mind. In countries, such as Nigeria, religious laws are being enacted in some Northern States, such as Zamfara, Kano, Jigawa, Katsina, Sokoto, Kebbi, Bauchi, Gombe, Borno, Yobe and Niger, where Sharia has been enshrined.

No wonder, Cardinal Francis Arinze, at one of his birthday ceremonies, called for a harmonious, peaceful coexistence arguing that "since there are more than one religion in the world, there is every need for all religious groups to tolerate each other's point of view and not to promote other agenda, such as total ethnic, economic, political, religious." Speaking at the same venue, former Catholic General Secretary, Rev. Fr. Matthew Hassan Kukah, identified corruption and ethnicity as the bane of peaceful existence in Nigeria. He cautioned against their misuse by fanatics to create anarchy in the society. He called for more dedication to God and service to mankind.

Religion, no doubt, plays an important role in the life of man, hence man's sentimental attraction to it.

Because of the centrality of religion in man's life, it occupies a prominent place in his actions and inactions. This includes how he reacts to perceived threats to his belief and how he propagates it. This has led to a lot of frictions among men, which has resulted in unpleasant developments, such as wars, riots, killings, and wholesale destruction of goods and property. Right from man's creation by God, he has been fighting one type of battle or the other over religion. Both the Christian scriptures and Muslim hadith contains stories of wars and uprising that took place in defense of religion For instance, the Bible tells us that Abraham fought with the kings of the neighboring nations (Genesis 14:1–16). The Hadith also records various wars fought by Prophet Muhammad (May Allah's peace be upon him) and his early followers. The Roman Emperors fought against the early church, while Nazi Germany eliminated over six million Jews because of racial and religious bigotry.

In the former Soviet Union and other communist states, it was a taboo for anyone to practice his religion in the open. Christianity was especially seen as an anathema, while Christians were randomly tortured for Christ, imprisoned, or murdered.

Bible and other religious literature were destroyed or outrightly banned by state decrees. Today, in states where there are state religions, such as Saudi Arabia, Libya, Iran, and Afghanistan, other religions are uniformly outlawed or suppressed. It is an offense by law to practice these religions. Punishments for disobedience are harshly cruel, and in some cases, attract the death penalty.

In Bosnia, Sudan, Indonesia, Syria, for instance, state terrorism has been unleashed against purported religious rivals organized by the state and implemented by organs of the state.

Thousands of people have lost their lives through such state-organized pogroms. Religious groups are not left out as they also organize premeditated attacks against their rivals resulting in bloodsheds and destruction.

In Nigeria, religious riots have become the order of the day. Intimidation and organized harassment by social miscreants and hoodlums occur from time to time.

In 1966, Nigeria fought a civil war, which was claimed to have been fought because of regional differences but with religious undertone. But the civil, war which the Federal Government of Nigeria claimed had "no victor, no vanquished," did not stop the spate of religious riots in the country up till today.

In 1980, religious riots broke out in the ancient Muslim city of Kano and thousands of lives were lost including destruction of properties. Few years later, it was the turn of Bulumkutu in Maiduguri where religious fanatics (BOKO HARAM) killed and destroyed at random. This group has turned out to be one of the deadliest terrorist groups in the world. Since then, no single year passes by without one form of religious crisis or the other rearing its horrible head in Nigeria.

In the case of Kano, religious crisis is a recurrent decimal.

Places, such as Kaduna, Zaria, Funtua, Bauchi, Gombe, Jos, and so on are becoming hotbeds of religious intolerance.

Despite declarations and declamations by governments and different religious groups themselves to seek lasting solution to these recurrent crises, nothing much has been achieved. The reason for this failure is the parties involved in these conflicts do not genuinely desire to end them and live and let live.

But religion should not be a do-or-die affair, for it is a personal matter between a man and his God. It is quite voluntary. It is the right of every man to choose the God he desires to serve and how he wants to serve him. No one has the right to force any belief on anybody including the constituted authority.

Conversion should be by persuasion and not by persecution. Everybody should be free to exercise his religious right without fear or favor. Religions should be allowed and encouraged to thrive side by side, harmoniously.

There should be a peaceful and enabling atmosphere for religious practice in every society. Individuals, groups, and even the government should not encourage religious animosity as this brings destabilization and retrogression.

Governments should hands-off in matters of religion and allow freedom of worship and association. Religion should be without rancor. Adherents of different religions should be able to coexist and worship their God without intimidation, in a peaceful environment.

Undue rivalry and suspicion should be discouraged and those involved in using religion to cause disharmony should be severely dealt with.

Governments should stop taking sides in religious matters affecting their people, and should not make laws that are against religions, especially when it affects a particular religion.

Religion should be given its rightful place in the society, whereby it is used as a vehicle for human development religion should be practiced in peace, without riots, for it to achieve its prime place in the affairs of men and nations. At Global Peace and Forgiveness Foundation, we believe that in the sight of God, real religion should uplift man and glorify God.

As the Bible puts it, "Pure religion and undefiled before God and the father is this: to visit the fatherless and widows in their affliction and to keep oneself unspotted from the world (James 1:27)."

Pure religion survives and thrives because it cures ills by not causing riots in the society for the good of all.

ETHNICITY WITHOUT ENMITY

"God regards all peoples and races as worthy of the same consideration."

—Pope Pius II

CAN RACIAL NATIONALITIES live together in concord and camaraderie without violating the ethics of emancipation and the paradigms of integration? Can ethnic communities live together in harmony and fraternity without recourse to rancor and violence? Can tribal entities live together in peace and understanding without intra and intertribal conflicts and cross swords?

The foregoing tripodal questions have become necessary in view of the demeaning racial disharmony, ethnic conflicts, and internecine tribal strifes that continue to agitate and ruffle the collective security of all lovers of peace and human dignity. The truth is that conflicts create diverse problems for all segments of society, leading, in most cases, to social disequilibrium and economic displacement.

In the study of "Ethnic Politics and the Persistence of Ethnic Identification," M. Parenti pointed that out to his constituency. Thus, ethnically salient parliamentary candidates tend to emerge and persist because of gains likely to accrue from appeals to ethnic sentiments. Arguing along the same line, R. Worlfinger said in "The Development and Persistence of Ethnic Voting" that "ethnicity provides one of the most convenient and appealing alternatives to [socio-economic program]. Political constituencies are often geographical in nature and quite often ethnically homogeneous."

The implication of the foregoing findings is that in "Africa, democracy promotes subnational ethnic demands capable of pitting ethnic groups one against another in strifes that can tear the country apart." Secondly, "the difficulty of an African opposition political party to justify its separate existence from the ruling party on the basis of some important and visible socio-economic program" accounts for disorientation from the opposition, which in most cases, only seeks for the downfall of the party in power.

What is more, the socio-economic competition among ethnic groups is fueled by multiparty political competition to create waste in the use of resources for development because of the political need to balance ethnic interests. Since ethnicity is seen as promoting the use of violence in multiparty competition, there is absence of restraints within the groups against the expression of hostility and violence toward out-group members. At the same time, in other to ensure group solidarity, individuals connive at injustices committed by co-ethnics and are willing to accept equity for other ethnic groups out of fear of being left behind in the interethnic scheme of things."

For the above-mentioned reasons, is there any wonder why multiparty democracy continues to suffer hiccups in multiethnic or plural societies in Africa? The impact of ethnicity on democracy has been considered negative in Africa, while multiparty democracy is seen to be essentially inappropriate. (From this prism, some analysts have argued in favor of one-party regime, as if this would provide any panacea to the situation.)

From the records, one party regime in Africa hardly fares better than multi-partyism. In many African countries, we can cite examples of experiments by General Acheampong Ghana's "Union Government," as well as proposals for no-party state, Afrocracy based on principles, norms, and morals of African traditional life, African socialism, which varies from Ujamaa in Tanzania to African welfare capitalism in Kenya, military rule modeled on the experience of Turkey under Prince Kemal Atarturk as well as Nigeria's two-party experiment under General Ibrahim Badamasi Babangida, then military president.

But it has been, and will continue to be argued with merit,

that ethnicity does not have negative impacts on democratic regime alone. Facts support existing evidences that in one party states, ethnic politics is used to manipulate and maneuver the party machinery.

In a paper presented on *Ethnicity, Class and the Struggle for State Power in Liberia* at a CODESRIA Conference on Ethnic in Africa, in Nairobi, Kenya, 1992, Professor

E. Osaghae, of Nigeria, noted that one way by which the true Whig party of Liberia managed to ward-off African-Liberian opposition to its rule was to collectively admit Afro-Liberians into the party and ensure that only those who were willing to play second fiddle climbed high in the party. He pointed out occasions when ethnicity created serious difficulties for African societies during non-democratic regimes. Such examples include the civil war Nigeria fought under the military from 1967–1970.

Others are the Marcias Nguema's rule in Equatorial Guinea, Jean Bedel Bokassa's in the Central African Republic, Idi Amin's in Uganda as well as the various military-imposed regimes and the escapades in Rwanda and Burundi, Eyadema in Togo, Mobutu in Zaire (now Democratic Republic of Congo), the civil wars in Angola, Sudan, Ethiopia, and ethno-racial massacres in Mauritania, which were characterized by the worst forms of ethnic violence perpetrated in extremely bizarre political systems and the authoritarian atmosphere.

But, despite the negative aspects of ethnicity, the question still arises whether it is possible for ethnic groups to live, move, and have their bearing in a climate devoid of mutual suspicion and enmity, especially in Africa? Granted, that this is possible, we now take a cursory look at the positive elements of ethnicity, and how these can be harnessed for more harmony, peace, forgiveness, and reconciliation in our world.

Historically, Africans are known to be their brother's keeper and neighbor's helper. Simon of Cyrene (an African), was there when Jesus of Nazareth could no longer bear the cross put on him by the Roman soldier-crucifers. He helped him out.

Despite the many iniquities visited on Nelson Mandela by the Dutch-Boer Apartheid regime in South Africa, he forgave them all when he was let off the hook after twenty-seven years of incarceration. This further proves the fact that the capacity of the African to forgive and forget is not only legendary but innate. Equally true is the value we place on hospitality as well as extended family care and concern, respect for elders, and the readiness to help those in need.

The positive impacts of ethnicity can lift the African over and above their negative aspects. First and foremost, "the political demands of many ethnic movements concern liberty and justice," according to Professor Okwudiba Nnoli of the University of Nigeria, Nsukka, who has advanced six points in support of ethnicity veritas.

First, he points out how through ethnicity, they express fears about the oppression of their members by other groups and about the nepotist distribution of public service jobs and social amenities, while the imposition of the culture of the dominant ethnic group on others insures that ethnicity contributes to democratic practice by its emphasis on equity and justice in socio-political relations.

Second, he argues that ethnicity leads to the appreciation of one's social roots in a community and cultural group, which is essential, not only for the stability of the individual and the ethnic group but that of the country as a whole.

Third, he argues that ethnicity provides a sense of belonging as part of an intermediate layer of social relations between the individual and the state.

Fourth, he maintains that ethnicity provided a local mobilization base for the anticolonial movement for national freedom.

Fifth, Nnoli, citing Osaghae, notes that ethnicity has been instrumental in the promotion of community development in the rural areas. He cited as an example, the rural- based ethnic unions which emerged in Liberia in the 1970s, with particular reference to SUSUKUU, a militant rural protest organization established by the Putu Development Corporation of Grand Gedeh County as work societies or cooperatives. Its radical opposition to incompetent governance had effects far beyond Putu chiefdom, for it contributed to the popular consciousness of the 1970s that dealt a death blow to the hegemony of the Americo-Liberians.

Another exceptional ethnic union in Liberia he cited was the Kru Corporation of Monrovia, which was registered in 1916 as a property-owning body. Apart from its judicial function of settling disputes among the Kru and the usual welfare functions, it participated actively in dock work affairs since most Krus and Monrovians were dock workers. Because of their abilities, the shipping companies placed a share of job assignments through the corporation. In 1958, it acted as a trade union in disputes with shipping companies.

Sixth, the mobilization of the various ethnic groups behind the various factions of a nations ruling class contributes to decentralization of power in the country. This is healthy for democratic reforms.

The late Rt. Honorable Dr. Nnamdi Azikiwe, first president of the Federal Republic of Nigeria, believed that the battle for existence and survival must carry with it a spirit and attitude of reconciliation even against one's implacable elements and opponents. He demonstrated this humanistic principle in his struggle against colonialism and in his accommodation of all Nigerians no matter their ethnic affiliation. Dr. Azikiwe, a pan-Africanist and friend of humanity, the Great Zik of Africa, considered racism and bigotry as an anathema to social intercourse.

In his philosophical eclecticism and pragmatism, Zik believed that tribalism can be contained within the sanctions of law and be utilized for the growth and development of society.

The effective management of ethnicity guarantees positive results and renders it legitimate. People can openly claim their ethnic identity without lessened esteem. They can even show that they are proud of their ethnic identity and seek redress from perceived official injustice or tyranny. Nations grow out of ethnic groups and the idea of national self-determination has its legitimacy in ethnicity.

As Ulf Bjorklund states in "Ethnicity and the Welfare State," the ideology of nationalism not only acts to legitimize truly national movements and aspirations, it also confers rationale and legitimacy on typical recent claims for ethnic equality and pluralism within modern states.

Also, R. Fox and his intellectual colleagues, have posited (in "Ethnic Nationalism and the Welfare State") that ethnic nationalism can best be explained as a new organization and ideological forum for political protest that occurs in welfare states as an alternative to and replacement for class-based forms of political opposition.

The salient feature of ethnic nationalism is its ability or attempt to bind local populations, differentiated by wealth, age, sex, education, residence, and even religion and language into a new political constituency seeking redress from the bureaucratic government. Ethnic groups can exist and function as brokers in the interstices between the state and the community. But they should be pervaded with a sense of goodwill, knowing fully well that "all men are created equal, that they are endowed by their Creator with certain inalienable right, and that among these are life, liberty, and the pursuit of happiness," as it is framed in the respected American constitution by sages and statesmen.

The first stanza of the first Nigeria National Anthem was equally couched in words epitomizing human empathy:

> "Nigeria we hail thee!
> Our own dear native land;
> Though tribe and tongue may differ,
> In brotherhood we stand
> Nigerians all are proud to serve
> Our own dear Motherland…"

The role of individuals toward enhancing ethnic harmony must also be stressed if this world is to be made a better place in which to live. When the Chinese philosopher, Confucius, realized that artificial affability does not suffer fools to be wise, he said, "Behave toward everyone as if receiving a great guest." Knowing that man's sojourn on earth is transitory and an odyssey of struggle, Stephen Grellet waxed poetic and resolved to be a friend to struggling humanity. In poetic equivocation, he echoed:

> I shall pass through this world but once;
> If, therefore, there be any kindness I can show,
> Or any good thing I can do,
> Let me do it now;
> Let me not differ it or neglect it,
> For I shall not pass this way again.

Since "our greatest good for humanity is in helping others help themselves," according to Sydney N. Bremer, "Let us learn to foster the bonds of brotherhood under the fatherhood of God."

POLITICS WITHOUT PROVOCATION

"We should play politics without bitterness, or rancor, or violence."

—Nwafor Orizu

THE GERMAN PHILOSOPHER of realism and power and an evolutionary doctrine of eternal struggle to dominate both environment and rival wills, Fredrick Wilhelm Nietzsche, once described politics in his famous doctrine of superman as "the art of reconciling rationally the irrationalities of man."

Politics is the game of power and has to do with authority—the power to assume a position and the authority to command that power, whether in terms of allocation of scarce resources or the exercise of state power. Put simply, politics has to do with resource control and allocation, the protection of certain interests, particularly partisan interests. It is because of the partisan nature of politics that competition and rivalry hold sway. Those who seek power, position, and authority believe that if they have these, they will influence their nations and fellow citizens, either for good or ill, for better for worse. Some enter politics with the clean aim of going for wealth, or to settle scores with their political foes. Yet, others play politics to promote ethic or national agenda, depending on their orientation and direction.

No matter how we look at it, politics is the vehicle to power, and without power, there can be no politics and vice-versa. It is therefore in the pursuit of power that people play politics. But rather than playing politics on the moral ground by joining issues, some people attack other people's personalities and question their very right to human existence. They play politics of provocation rather than politics of reconciliation, but by playing the politics of personality cults, they end up with personality crisis. Nations have gone to war because of the political interest of a person or group of persons. Examples abound of how kings were deposed and monarchies routed, because of the political agenda of rival groups. In the civilized nations of the world, politics is played on vital issues of the state interest-matters that will help the citizenry. Politicians in civilized nations speak on how to uplift the general well-being on the commonwealth of their fellow citizens. But apart from speaking on the good for the people, when they get power, such politicians work to ensure that the people, their people are not forgotten. Developmental projects are embarked upon for the common good.

In less civilized nations of the world, politics is played as a dirty game, as a shortcut to amass primitive wealth, to create social and religious chaos. In such societies, man lives in a state of nature, where life is short and brutish.

Speaking during Nigeria's Second Republic, Late Alhaji Waziri Ibrahim, leader of the defunct Great Nigeria People's Party (GNPP) advised politicians to adopt the spirit of tolerance, accommodation and peaceful coexistence in the interest of unity. Using Nwafor Orizu's phrase, "Politics without bitterness," was employed as his party's slogan.

This message is indeed relevant in Nigeria's body polity. It should not be directed to practicing politicians alone but to all stake holders in the system.

Politics refers to matters concerned with acquiring or exercising power within a group or an organization. This can be either at the local, state, national, or international levels. Since the time of Aristotle, man has been described as a political animal.

His participation in the affairs of his community is his duty. People go into politics for different reasons. For whatever reason, a man goes into politics, the intention is to promote an interest. The interest may be personal, sectional, or national in nature.

Politics has been existing and has been part of man right

from the beginning of his sojourn on earth. It is the very basis of his existence. Everything man does is centered on politics.

He cannot divorce himself from it because whatever he does has political connotations. In the larger society, every decision taken by those in authority, whether he was consulted or not, affects him. People participate in politics as supporters, sympathizers, or activists. In fact, everyone has a role to play in politics. It is a team event, necessitating team spirit.

How politics is played in a society really deter- mines how that society will be. Its future is determined by the type of politics it plays. Politics can be played along ideological, religious, tribal, or even nationalistic lines.

For example, the former USSR, People's Republic of China, Democratic People's Republic of Korea, and Cuba have communism as their political ideology, while Britain, USA, France, Germany, India, and Nigeria practice capitalism in their democracies.

Some countries, such as Saudi Arabia, Libya, and Iran, use Islam as a religious legal code with Sharia as an ideology and mode of governance. Countries such as Switzerland and Lesotho are kingdoms ruled by the monarchy.

Whatever mode of governance a society has decided to adopt as his method of government, it is expected that the means and method to achieve this should be through a level playing ground, fairness, equal opportunity, nonviolence, peaceful coexistence, tolerance, mutual respect, and good sportsmanship. Above all, there should be the fear of God.

In every society, whatever is the mode of governance or ideology, there must be opposing views. People are not made by nature to think alike or to agree along the same lines all the time, even among people of the same grouping there must be dissenting or supporting views in every action or inaction in a society even by the same people on whose behalf decisions are taking. This can also happen among members of the same political group.

Dissension is an integral part of politics. If there is no dissension or opposition in politics, there will not be a healthy growth in the political system. Nations that have tolerated political differences and ideologies and have allowed time to nurture their political processes are now reaping the gains of stable and progressive governments—the United States, Great Britain, France, Germany, Switzerland, Netherlands, etc., are ready examples, while those that have sponsored political intolerance and anarchy have gone the way of the dogs (i.e., destruction and disintegration). They include Yugoslavia, Czechoslovakia as well as Burundi, and Rwanda in Africa.

The need for political tolerance among contending political forces cannot be overemphasized. In Nigeria for instance, the country gained independence in 1960 and has had four republics, with over thirty years of military rule, yet the spirit of intolerance and politics of provocation has sent its democratic gains to the marines.

In 1964, when the United Progressive People Grand Alliance (UPPGA) held their national convention in Jos, members of the opposition parties attacked their members, and this action led to loss of lives and properties.

In the so-called "Wild Wild West" of the 1960's, political intolerance and provocation led to widespread civil unrest and the eventual collapse of Nigeria's First Republic.

During the second republic, political intolerance, deliberate falsehood, blackmail, provocation, and intimidation were the order of the day, while corruption and other vices helped to hasten the collapse of the second republic. Also during the General Ibrahim Babandiga's regime, the annulment of a democratically conducted elections by the military, led to a prolonged period of sabre-rattling, political intolerance, brinksmanship, deliberate falsehood, blackmail, and deliberate provocation of one part of the country by another.

These actions could have led to the disintegration of Nigeria, but for God's divine intervention. Now that the country is in its fourth experiment of democracy, the politicians and their supporters seem not to have learnt their lesson as political banditry, undue provocation, and outright murder of members of the opposition are the order of the day.

Since the inception of the Fourth Republic in Nigeria, the urge to be in absolute control by contending political forces has so heated the body polity, and one begins to wonder if Nigeria has learnt their lessons from events of the past. Nigeria has agreed that the worst democratic government is better than the best military government. Yet, while this assertion is born from experience, some politicians seem to be playing to the gallery. It is the duty of the politicians to oversee governance during the democratic regimes, and they can accomplish this through elections. While seeking power, politicians are involved in electioneering campaigns and other forms of activities that may lead to their success at the polls, either for themselves, party, or candidates.

As earlier mentioned, because of intolerance and undue rivalry, the political class has turned politics and governance to a do-or-die affair. Discipline and decorum are in short supply in the body polity. Even in or out of government, politicians and their supporters have made the art of politicking a deadly and expensive affair. They have turned politics into a dog-eat-dog monstrosity.

It is not supposed to be so. Politics is an art. It is an art concerned with the seeking, acquiring, and exercising of power, and when it is played according to the rules, it becomes quite interesting and rewarding.

The rules in the game of politics are tolerance, give-and-take, maturity, honesty, determination, fairness, good sportsmanship, and fear of God. Politicians and their supporters should endeavor to play the game of politics according to the rules and to always avoid provoking their opponents by their actions, to avoid the mistakes of the past and their terrible consequences.

Politicians should play the game of politics without provocation, and by the grace of God, we shall arrive at the Promised Land.

SOVEREIGNTY STANDS ON STABILITY

"Political sovereignty is but a mockery without the means of meeting poverty and illiteracy and disease. Self-determination is but a slogan if the future holds no hope."

—John F. Kennedy

THERE IS NO DOUBT that all the nations of the world are proud of their dignity and sovereignty. They are jealous of their status because their nations are theirs to uphold, to build, to defend, to live for, and if need be, die for.

No nation on earth, no matter how big or small, is ready to barter away its sovereignty to another nation, no matter the attractions or wealth of such another. Rather, the fact needs emphasizing that every nation is proud of its sovereign status, with defined geographical and territorial boundaries.

In political science, sovereignty refers to the ultimate overseer or authority in the decision-making process of the state and in the maintenance of order. It also means the absolute right of an independent nation to make war or peace and sign treaties with other states free of external control. The concept of sovereignty in both political theory and international law is closely related to the concepts of state and government, of independence and democracy. Originally, as derived from the Latin term *superanus* and the French term *souvrainete*, sovereignty was meant to be the equivalent of supreme power. But this definition is no longer applicable, having departed from its traditional rendition.

The history of sovereignty can be traced to sixteenth century France, when Jean Bodin used the new concept to bolster the power of the French king over rebellious feudal lords, thereby facilitating the transition from feudalism to nationalism. The theories of John Locke (seventeenth century) and Jean-Jacques Rousseau (eighteenth century), posited that "the State is based upon a compact of its citizens, through which they entrust such powers to a government as may be necessary for common protection." This led to the development of popular sovereignty that found expression in the United States Declaration of Independence in 1776. The idea of popular sovereignty exercised primarily by the people became thus combined with the idea of national sovereignty exercised not by an unorganized people in the state of nature but a nation embodied in an organized state.

In every nation of the world, there is a constitution, whether written or unwritten, which often upholds sovereignty. While the doctrine of sovereignty has had an important impact on developments within states, its greatest influence has been in the relations between states. Bodin ascribes sovereignty as "common to all nations (*jus gentium*)" as well as the fundamental laws of the state. The Charter of the United Nations recognizes and emphasizes the sovereignty of members' states, when it states, "The principle of sovereign equality of all its members." Because of this principle and recognition, the UN accords equal voting right to all member states at its General Assembly.

In consequences, of the above developments, sovereignty has ceased to be considered as synonymous with unrestricted power. States have accepted a considerable body of law, limiting their sovereign right of acting as they please. In this way, a delicate balance has been achieved between the needs of the international society and the desire of states to protect their sovereignty to the maximum possible extent. Granted if sovereignty gives states freedom from external control, how can they (states) be stable internally, economically, socially, and politically? What of the internal contractions that tend to threaten the sovereignty of states, especially when there are "divided loyalties" and "divided sovereignty"? We believe that nations can have stability internally when there is good governance, justice, and peace.

The late Sardauna of Sokoto and premier of Northern Nigeria, Sir Ahmadu Bello had the idea of good governance in mind when he said,

> "Our aims were very simple. To develop the country (Nigeria) to the fullest extent in the shortest time, to preserve the peace, good order, and friendly relations with all our different people, to conduct efficient and impartial administration, to ensure for all, freedom of thought, and religion, to do good to all men."

For the nations of the world to enjoy their sovereignty, they must cling to spiritual stability. This means that citizens of every country must embrace spiritual verities, such as stability of character, integrity, honesty, freedom of thought, freedom of expression, and freedom of assembly. Add economic stability and political stability to the fore-going, and a new era of freedom will dawn on humanity. Freedom! This is a wonderful word. Since the creation of man by God, he has always been fighting one important battle. That is the battle to be free. The battle for freedom has not been easy for man as he has both nature and other odds against him. Individually and collectively, man has organized himself into a formidable force with the sole aim of freeing himself from perceived bondage created for him by fellow man or circumstances.

Right from existence of man on earth, he has always desired to be free to live the type of life he has chosen for himself. Unfortunately, this has not been possible, because of forces beyond his control. Despite these odds, however, man has not given up the desire to be free. In other to achieve freedom, man has used every available means to free himself from whatsoever he feels keeps him in bondage. From experience, man knows that he alone will not be able to achieve freedom, so he decided to ally himself with other men to achieve this purpose. He did this through the forming of associations or groups with political or cultural bias. Through this association, he can express his wish to be free and also to apply whatever means he deems fit to achieve his freedom.

After obtaining freedom, man decided to transfer this freedom into the hands of an individual or group of individuals to take care and control on his behalf. This he did in form of government or sovereign, but sovereignty belongs to the people, especially in democracies. In most cases, the fight for freedom, which leads to sovereignty was fought and won by the people, who in turn hand over their sovereignty to an individual or group to oversee their affairs indefinitely or for a period, thus the slogan "power belongs to the people." Without sovereignty, there will be no power. Whatever is the type of government that holds power on behalf of the people, whether it's a monarchy, democracy, or dictatorship, what brings success to its sovereignty is stability and personal freedom.

The Quran guarantees personal freedom—freedom of choice. But the Muslim conservatives in countries, such as Iran, old Iraq, and Indonesia see to it that people are denied this freedom because of the hidden agenda of those who want to keep their people under bondage. But despite of the hardline postures of hardline conservatives, their citizens are clamoring and voting for freedom of political expression. They are voting for reform and freedom.

The press is in the vanguard of this social crusade for freedom in order to avert an explosion. Democracy in Iran is being bred in newspaper journalism, as brave journalists battle for freedom of expression. And they are winning because the backbone of independent press can mobilize public opinion against unpopular regimes. The press has got social power against political power. A vibrant press in the hands of a new generation of reformers, who can stand?

The four estates of the realm can create stability for the sovereignty of a country, provided those who hold the reins of power do not antagonize those who belong to the fraternity of the pen, through repression and high-handedness. At Global Peace and Forgiveness Foundation, we believe that sovereignty stands on stability. Without stability, there is no way a sovereign can exercise his sovereign powers. It will be like fish out of water. Everybody cherishes freedom and to maintain freedom, there is need for stability.

Countries, such as USA, Britain, France, Japan, and Germany have achieved peace and development because of stability in the polity. Some past world leaders, such as Mansa Kankan Musa of The Old Mali Empire, late president Tito of Yugoslavia, Humphrey Boigny of Ivory Coast, and Sekou Toure of Guinea, were able to bring stability to their various countries and governments by appealing to creative energies of their citizens. Thus, there was peace, progress, and advancement in their countries, in their time. The former president of South Africa, Nelson Mandela, is another symbol of stability. With his reputation and influence, he was able to bring together the people of South Africa despite their ethnic and racial differences and placed their sovereignty on the path of justice, growth, and national cohesion. The need for stability on the body polity in any given nation is important to its corporate existence. Evidence has proved that nations that thread the part of instability always end up in destruction and disintegration due to inability to sustain their sovereignty. A living example is Somalia where a decade of anarchy has reduced it to rubbles. The panacea for development of any nation is the stability of its sovereignty.

Right from independence of nation states, the need for stability has always been the most significant aspect of the objectives of those in charge of government. The government consolidates its powers immediately it comes into office by involving and talking care of various groups and their interests. It provides an atmosphere for peace and stability and establishes the authority of sovereign state and creates room for the sustenance of its sovereignty.

Without a solid foundation based on, among others, the respect of the rights of the people and regard for the rule of law, no government whatsoever its source of power, will be able to bring stability to bear on its sovereignty. Rather such a government will wallow in the gallows of anarchy. Peace will elude it, and the country will remain in turmoil and underdevelopment. Even what has been achieved by previous government will be destroyed.

The late President Felix Humphrey Boigny of Ivory Coast, right from his country's independence, provided an atmosphere for peace and stability in the polity through good governance and respect for human right. This led to rapid development that made Ivory Coast a stable economy in West Africa. Sad to say, this is no longer so, as strife and anarchy have overtaken the country, even as this book is being written. President Fidel Castro of Cuba, despite the odds against him and the people of Cuba, has been able to maintain stability in the sovereignty of his country, and this has led to peace, progress, and development.

Notwithstanding the mode of or type of government being operated in any country, the need for stability is paramount, and it is the most important ingredient for its survival. For a country to fail, all its enemies need to do is to promote instability into the system, and the country will reel into disintegration.

Governments and peoples need to encourage stability in their countries through peaceful coexistence, tolerance, good government, hard work, respect for the rule of law and human rights. They should promote economic benefits for the citizens as well as social, political, cultural, religious, and ethnic harmonies that will rebound to stability, peace, progress, and development.

Can countries such as Somalia, Sudan, Burundi, Rwanda, Democratic Republic of Congo, Afghanistan, Ivory Coast compare with countries such as Japan, Malaysia, Singapore Taiwan, and others that are enjoying and reaping the fruits of stability?

All the countries in the world cannot enjoy the benefits of stability until they seek peace, forgiveness, understanding, and reconciliation, which are the basis for political and economic development. Political and economic development can only be achieved in an atmosphere of peace and stability, for these create room for good governance and healthy competition among various groups in the system.

It is the responsibility of the government and the people of a country to promote and protect values that promote peace and stability. When those concerned are aware of this responsibility and perform it accordingly, peace and progress are the benefits thereof. The twenty-first century is the century for development, and no individual or nation should be left behind in this profitable venture. It is a time for everyone to reap the benefits of industrialization, computerization, and information technology.

Everybody succeeds in an atmosphere of peace and stability, while only the devil succeeds in war, anarchy, and wanton destruction. The world needs peace and stability, and only the people of the world can give it to her. Give peace a chance, and there will be progress and development.

THE WORLD OF PEACE, FORGIVENESS AND RECONCILIATION

"Peace is rarely denied to the peaceful."
—Johann von Schiller

BLESSED ARE THE peacemakers, for they shall be called the children of God. Jesus Christ pronounces benediction on all the lovers and workers of peace because he knows the value of peace. In another place, he commands and commends, "Peace on earth, goodwill toward men," because he wants men to live in peace on planet earth.

All the world today prays for the time to come when men "shall beat their swords into ploughshares and their spears into pruning hooks," when nation shall not lift up sword against nation, neither shall they learn war anymore." Those who disturb peace on earth are the "black sheep," who have gone astray from the flock, bringing distraction and destruction upon individuals and nations to further their ambition, malice, or revenge. But the whole world will be at peace when the majority become truly circumcised in heart and put on the heart of flesh, not of stone and become really civilized. We may think we are civilized, and even call ourselves civilized, but strife, conflict and violence all around us prove our erroneous assertion.

No wonder, a lover of peace, J. W. Dickson once said, "War is but our bastard inheritance of barbarism, and it will be called the golden age that finds a way to rid the earth of this unspeakable crime against humanity wars of aggression."

Presently, the global affront against terrorism is a welcome development, seeing that peace is a basic requirement for human progress.

So concerned was Dag Hammarskjold, a onetime Secretary-General of the United Nations (1953-1961), about a world bereft of peace that he lamented, "We have tried so hard, and we have failed so miserably. I see no hope for world permanent peace. Unless the world has a spiritual rebirth in the next few years, civilization is doomed."

Those who work against peace are bound to doom civilization because they are agents of destruction.

Is the world putting emphasis on the right things today?

Why are the issues of peace, forgiveness, and reconciliation not as popular as their negative counterparts of war, vengeance, and retaliation? We need to ponder on the imperatives of those positive elements that unite to advance human civilization and advancement.

If the world can create a fresh atmosphere of peace for the rechanneling of the enormous resources available to nation states, the future will look bright, not bleak. If the world can heal the wounds of nations through united prayers, peace will become a new reality. If the world can learn to prepare for peace rather than war, there will be room for reconciliation, even between enemies.

The need to return to God is vital and urgent for those who want to impact on their generation positively. As the first president of the United States, George Washington stated, "It is impossible to rightly govern the world without God and the Bible."

God is important, and he rules in the affairs of men. What is beyond the ken of human understanding is easy before God. God is omnipotent, omniscient, and omnipresent. He is the First, and he is the Last, and besides him, there is no other.

God is eternal, and his righteousness endures forever. God is absolutely in a class by himself, absolutely sui generi.

God is ens premum, depending on no one for his existence and having everything else dependent upon him for its existence. Furthermore, God is ens omnium excellenissimum, the most exalted being that whom no better being can possibly exist or be imagined.

Are there some lost sheep in garbs of atheism and

agnosticism who doubt the existence of God? We refer such individuals to the following passages in the Holy Writ:

> "The heavens declare the glory of God, and the firmament shows his handwork. Day unto day utters speech and night unto night reveals knowledge. There is no speech or language where their voice is not heard (Psalm19:1–3).
>
> "O Lord, how manifold are your works! In wisdom, you have made them all. The earth is full of your possessions. (Psalm104:24)."
>
> "And he has made from one blood every nation of men to dwell on the surface of the earth and has determined their pre-appointed times and the boundaries of their dwellings. So that they should seek the Lord in the hope that they might grope for him and find him, though he is not far from each of us; for in him, we live and move and have our being (Acts 17:26–28)." As also some of your own poets have said, "For we are also his offsprings."
>
> "For the wrath of God is revealed from heaven against all ungodliness and unrighteousness of men, who suppress the truth in unrighteousness, because what may be known of God is manifest in them, for God has shown it to them. For since the creation of the world his invisible attributes are clearly seen, being understood by the things that are made, even his eternal power and Godhead (Romans 1:18–20)."

God is required in the question of peace, forgiveness and reconciliation because by man's nature, he is not peaceful; man will find it easier to seek peace and pursue it, to forgive and be forgiven, and to reconcile with his neighbor. The power of prayer has been known to heal not only individuals but groups, communities, and nations. God is no respecter of persons, and those who call upon him with a sincerity of heart, irrespective of their race, sex, creed, educational background, or status in life, are ever assured of divine response. This much the Bible says, accordingly to the following passage:

> "If my people who are called by My name will humble themselves and pray and seek My face, and turn away from their wicked ways, then I will hear from heaven and will forgive their sin and heal their land (2 Chronicles 7:14)."

God's condition for forgiveness includes humility, prayer, and repentance. The nations of the world today need all these three to enjoy divine protection from the Creator of the universe himself. At Global Peace and Forgiveness Foundation, we recommend prayer as a way of life because its efficacy is boundless. We therefore urge daily, constant, and regular prayers for world peace, national stability, and those in authority.

We also urge prayers for personal repentance and forgiveness from God and one another. The grace to tolerate and forgive one another will be given to nation groups, if prayers are made with purpose. As Colossians 3:13 admonishes, "Bear with each other and forgive whatever grievances you may have against one another."

Furthermore, there is every need for us all to pray for the restoration of our nations, to pray against satanic forces, and for the covenant of peace, as taught by Ezekiel the Evangelist:

> "I will make a covenant of peace with them and rid the land of wild beasts so that they may live in the desert and sleep in the forests for safety. I will bless them and the places surrounding my hill. I will send down showers in season; there will be showers of blessing. The trees of the field will yield its crops, and the people will be secured in their land. They will know that I am the Lord, when I break the bars of their yoke and rescue them from the hands of those who enslaved them. They will no longer be plundered by the nations, nor will wild animals devour them. They will live in safety, and no one will make them afraid (Ezekiel 34:25–28)."

In line with the needs for intercessory prayer, we counsel Christians to pray for people of all other faiths. Across the world, we advise Christians to pray especially for Muslims, as we urge Muslims to pray especially for Christians. With united prayers for each other, Christians and Muslims will become positive agents of *change* in the world.

In the same vein, we call on Hindus, Taoists, Zoroastrians, and people of other creeds to pray for those outside their faith. Religion, ideally, should be complementary, not competitive. It is the blind faith of those who think that they are the only ones who know God, who have become fundamentalists and fanatics in the religious arena. Otherwise, religion can be used as a channel of blessing and development if those who profess it abide by its tenets and teaching for good.

The vision for a genuine *reconciliation* cannot be realized if the art of *forgiveness* is not embraced holistically. The father of peace is justice, while the mother of justice is forgiveness. But being a personal matter, forgiveness is both a decision and a process. It takes a personal decision to forgive even ourselves. The "permission" to forgive must therefore stem from within and granted without, for it to become a reality.

Forgiveness is a step to reconciliation. Forgiveness is holistic, and prayer is a part of the process of forgiveness. At times, the pains of the past hurts continue to linger in us and color our behavior toward those who hurt us. Some of such hurts may be results of events that happened even before we were born (such as family feuds or ancestral curses). But with the iodine of forgiveness, there is hope for reconciliation. That is why when it seems most difficult to forgive, we must necessarily resort to prayer.

Forgiveness is the letting go of any desire for revenge. While it does not claim the nonexistence of hurt, injustice, infringement, or manipulation, the spirit of forgiveness nevertheless brings to bear a clear understanding of human frailty. Once the dictum "To err is human" becomes our ethos, we shall appreciate the maxim "To forgive is divine" in clearer perspective. The understanding of this virtue can induce a fresh relationship at all levels in every given society. Reconciliation, on the other hand, is a process through which those affected sink their differences and express enough new mutual trust to come together and ask themselves for forgiveness. Reconciliation is a product of letting go and letting God, of live and let live, of give-and-take. It is premised on "no winner, no loser," "no victor, no vanquished."

That is why we need to turn a new leaf and heed the biblical injunction: "A new heart also will I give you, and a new spirit will I put within you, and I take away the stony heart out of your flesh, and I will give an heart of flesh (Ezekiel 36:26)." The world needs to say "YES" to God.

This is the best way to promote peace, forgiveness, and reconciliation, while affecting humanity positively with divinity and dignity, on planet earth.

Photo Gallery of Global Peace and Forgiveness Foundation in Nigeria

ND NATIONAL FORGIVENESS DAY CELEBRATION
GLOBAL PEACE & FORGIVENESS FOUNDATION (NGO)
IN COLLABORATION WITH
NATIONAL ORIENTATION AGENCY (NOA)
PUBLIC COMPLAINTS COMMISSION (PCC)
SPECIAL GUEST OF HONOUR
HER EXCELLENCY, CHIEF MRS. STELLA OBASANJO,
SEPTEMBER 25, 2004
AREA 3 GARKI, ABUJA.

2ND NATIONAL FORGIVENESS DAY CELEBRATION

SWAN

NATIONAL FORGIVENESS DAY CELEBRATION
HER EXCELLENCY, CHIEF MRS. STELLA OBASANJO,

AMBROSE ALLI UNIVERSITY CHAPTER
THE NEED FOR PEACE

PEACE & FORGIVEN
FOUNDATION
1ST NATIONAL
DAY
PEACE, FORGIVEN
RECONCILIATION"
OKOROCHA
JERRY GANA

2ND NATIONAL FORGIVENESS DAY CELEBRATION
NATIONAL ORIENTATION AGENCY (NOA)
PUBLIC COMPLAINTS COMMISSION (PCC)

WORLDWIDE FORGIVENESS ALLIANCE

The Board of Directors hereby honors

PATRICK EGBERUARE

Champion of Forgiveness

In recognition of his courage and commitment to forgiveness, peace and reconciliation.

On this day, August 3, 2014

Robert W. Plath
Founder & President

REFERENCES

Arthur Beales, History of Peace, 1931.

Nwankwo, Arthur. *Emancipation as a Paradigm*. Nigeria:

Fourth Dimension Pub. Co, 1996.

Claude Ake, the "*African Context of Human Rights*" in Africa Today, Vol 3, Nos 1&2, 1987.

David Thomson, *Europe Since Napoleon*, 1977. Dictionary of Quotations

Horowitz, Donald. *Ethnic Groups in Conflict*. Berkley and Los Angeles, California: University of California Press, Ltd, 1985.

E. Osaghae, "Ethnicity, Class and the Struggle for Sate Power in Liberia", Paper Presented at a CODESRIA Conference on Ethnic Conflict in Africa, Nairobi Kenya, November, 1992 [Ibid] " Do Ethnic Minorities Still Exist in Nigeria"? I*n the Journal of Common-Wealth and comparative Politics*, Vol. 249 No 2, July 1986.

J. A Wiseman, *Democracy in Black Africa*, Paragon House, New York.

Joseph Flavious, "The Antiquity of Jews" in Josephus: *The Complete Works,* translated and edited by William Whiston, 1737.

J. S Coleman: *Nigeria: Background to Nationalism* (Berkeley, University of California Press), 1958.

Lawrence S. Wittner, *Rebels Against War*: The American Peace Movement, 1933–1984, (Temple University Press, 1984).

M. Parenti, "Ethnic Politics and the Persistence of Ethnic Identification", *American Political Science Review*, Vol. ix, No.4, 1967.

Morton A. Kaplan, *Consolidating Peace in Europe*

Nnamdi Obasi, *Ethnic Militias, Vigilante Groups and Separatist Movements in Nigeria.*

Okudiba Nnoli; *Ethnicity and Democracy in Africa*, Malthouse Press Ltd, Lagos, Nigeria, 1994.

15. R. Fox etal: *"Ethnic Nationalism and the Welfare State"* C. Keyes ed. Ethnic Change (Seattle University of Washington Press), 1981

R. Wolfinger, "The development and Persistence of Ethnic Voting", in American Political Science Review, Vol. Lix, No. 4, 1965.

Uef Bjorkland "*Ethnicity and the welfare State*" *in international Social Science Journal. February 1987.*

Reggae Legend: Bob Marley Lyrics

All Scriptural References are from Holy Bible. King James Version and the New King James Version

All Islamic Inferences are from the Noble Quran and Hadith.

Research Aid from *Wagna & Funk Encyclopedias*, etc.

www.ingramcontent.com/pod-product-compliance
Lightning Source LLC
Chambersburg PA
CBHW060909280326
41934CB00007B/1251

* 9 7 8 0 5 7 8 7 6 3 5 9 0 *